Workshop on Semantic Search 2010

Held at NAACL HLT 2010

Los Angeles, California, USA
5 June 2010

ISBN: 978-1-61738-681-7

Printed from e-media with permission by:

Curran Associates, Inc.
57 Morehouse Lane
Red Hook, NY 12571

Some format issues inherent in the e-media version may also appear in this print version.

Printed by Curran Associates, Inc. (2010)

For permission requests, please contact the Association for Computational Linguistics at the address below.

Association for Computational Linguistics
209 N. Eighth Street
Stroudsburg, Pennsylvania 18360

Phone: 1-570-476-8006
Fax: 1-570-476-0860

acl@aclweb.org

Additional copies of this publication are available from:

Curran Associates, Inc.
57 Morehouse Lane
Red Hook, NY 12571 USA
Phone: 845-758-0400
Fax: 845-758-2634
Email: curran@proceedings.com
Web: www.proceedings.com

Introduction

Welcome to the NAACL HLT Workshop on Semantic Search!

Information retrieval (IR) research has been actively driven by the challenging information overload problem and many successful general-purpose commercial search engines. While the popularity of the largest search engines is a confirmation of the success and utility of IR, the identification, representation, and use of the often-complex semantics behind user queries has not yet been fully explored.

In this workshop we target methods that exploit semantics in search-related tasks. One of the major obstacles in bridging the gap between IR and Natural Language Processing (NLP) is how to retain the flexibility and precision of working with text at the lexical level while gaining the greater descriptive precision that NLP provides. We have solicited contributions on automatic analysis of queries and documents in order to encode and exploit information beyond surface-level keywords: named entities, relations, semantic roles, etc.

This workshop is meant to accelerate the pace of progress in semantic search techniques by connecting IR and NLP, bridging semantic analysis and search methodologies, and exploring the potentials of search utilizing semantics. We also focus on forming an interest group from different areas of research, exploring collaboration opportunities, providing deeper insight into bringing semantics into search, and provoking or encouraging discussions on all of its potential.

We are interested in semantic search technologies including the following topics:
- Query Parsing and Semantic Tagging
- Query Suggestion and Recommendation
- Query Expansion and Intention Detection
- Web Query Analysis and Mining
- Semantic Annotation and Indexing
- Language Modeling for Information Retrieval
- Information Extraction and Summarization for Indexing and Search
- Question Answering
- Search Reranking Integrating Semantic Features
- Search Relevance Evaluation using Semantic Technology
- Topic Modeling and Semantic Tagging

We received 11 submissions and selected 6 papers after a rigorous review process. Each paper has been reviewed by at least three reviewers. We are pleased to present these papers in this volume.

Our workshop will start with a keynote speech by Ronald Kaplan (Powerset Division of Microsoft Bing). We will also hold a panel discussion on the potential to explore semantic search technologies.

We are very grateful to the Program Committee for their hard work, and the presenters for their excellent papers.

Best regards,
Donghui Feng, Jamie Callan, Eduard Hovy, and Marius Paşca
Workshop Organizers

Organizers:

Donghui Feng, AT&T Interactive
Jamie Callan, Carnegie Mellon University
Eduard Hovy, USC/Information Sciences Institute
Marius Paşca, Google Inc.

Program Committee:

Srinivas Bangalore, AT&T Labs-Research
Raman Chandrasekar, Microsoft Research
Jennifer Chu-Carroll, IBM Research
Nikesh Garera, Kosmix
Ralph Grishman, New York University
Patrick Haffner, AT&T Labs-Research
Liang Huang, USC/Information Sciences Institute
Heng Ji, City University of New York
Zornitsa Kozareva, USC/Information Sciences Institute
Hang Li, Microsoft Research Asia
Dekang Lin, Google Inc.
Yumao Lu, Yahoo! Labs
Hwee Tou Ng, National University of Singapore
Fuchun Peng, Yahoo! Labs
Ellen Riloff, University of Utah
Dan Roth, University of Illinois at Urbana-Champaign
James Shanahan, AT&T Interactive
Young-In Song, Microsoft Research Asia
Qin Wang, AT&T Interactive
Kenji Yamada, AT&T Interactive
Remi Zajac, AT&T Interactive

Invited Speaker:

Ronald Kaplan, Powerset Division of Microsoft Bing

Table of Contents

Workshop Program

Saturday, June 5, 2010

9:20-9:30 Opening Remarks

9:30-10:30 Invited Talk by Ronald Kaplan

10:30-11:00 Morning Break

11:00–11:30 *LDA Based Similarity Modeling for Question Answering*
Asli Celikyilmaz, Dilek Hakkani-Tur and Gokhan Tur

11:30–12:00 *Experts' Retrieval with Multiword-Enhanced Author Topic Model*
Nikhil Johri, Dan Roth and Yuancheng Tu

12:00–12:30 *Query-based Text Normalization Selection Models for Enhanced Retrieval Accuracy*
Si-Chi Chin, Rhonda DeCook, W. Nick Street and David Eichmann

12:30-1:45 Lunch Break

1:45–2:15 *A Graph-Based Semi-Supervised Learning for Question Semantic Labeling*
Asli Celikyilmaz and Dilek Hakkani-Tur

2:15-3:00 Panel Discussion

3:00-3:30 Afternoon Break

3:30–3:45 *Capturing the Stars: Predicting Ratings for Service and Product Reviews*
Narendra Gupta, Giuseppe Di Fabbrizio and Patrick Haffner

3:45–4:00 *Object Search: Supporting Structured Queries in Web Search Engines*
Kim Pham, Nicholas Rizzolo, Kevin Small, Kevin Chen-Chuan Chang and Dan Roth

4:00-4:45 Workshop Wrap-up Discussion

LDA Based Similarity Modeling for Question Answering

Asli Celikyilmaz
Computer Science Department
University of California, Berkeley
asli@eecs.berkeley.edu

Dilek Hakkani-Tur
International Computer
Science Institute
Berkeley, CA
dilek@icsi.berkeley.edu

Gokhan Tur
Speech Technology and
Research Laboratory
SRI International
Menlo Park, CA, USA
gokhan@speech.sri.com

Abstract

We present an exploration of generative modeling for the question answering (QA) task to rank candidate passages. We investigate Latent Dirichlet Allocation (LDA) models to obtain ranking scores based on a novel similarity measure between a natural language question posed by the user and a candidate passage. We construct two models each one introducing deeper evaluations on latent characteristics of passages together with given question. With the new representation of topical structures on QA datasets, using a limited amount of world knowledge, we show improvements on performance of a QA ranking system.

1 Introduction

Question Answering (QA) is a task of automatic retrieval of an answer given a question. Typically the question is linguistically processed and search phrases are extracted, which are then used to retrieve the candidate documents, passages or sentences.

A typical QA system has a pipeline structure starting from extraction of candidate sentences to ranking true answers. Some approaches to QA use keyword-based techniques to locate candidate passages/sentences in the retrieved documents and then filter based on the presence of the desired answer type in candidate text. Ranking is then done using syntactic features to characterize similarity to query. In cases where simple question formulation is not satisfactory, many advanced QA systems implement more sophisticated syntactic, semantic and contextual processing such as named-entity recognition (Molla et al., 2006), coreference resolution (Vicedo and Ferrandez, 2000), logical inferences (abduction or entailment) (Harabagiu and Hickl, 2006) translation (Ma and McKeowon, 2009), etc., to improve answer ranking. For instance, *how* questions, or spatially constrained questions, etc., require such types of deeper understanding of the question and the retrieved documents/passages.

Many studies on QA have focused on discriminative models to predict a function of matching features between each question and candidate passage (set of sentences), namely **q/a pairs**, e.g., (Ng et al., 2001; Echihabi and Marcu, 2003; Harabagiu and Hickl, 2006; Shen and Klakow, 2006; Celikyilmaz et al., 2009). Despite their success, they have some room for improvement which are not usually raised, e.g., they require hand engineered features; or cascade features learnt separately from other modules in a QA pipeline, thus propagating errors. The structures to be learned can become more complex than the amount of training data, e.g., alignment, entailment, translation, etc. In such cases, other source of information, e.g., unlabeled examples, or human prior knowledge, should be used to improve performance. Generative modeling is a way of encoding this additional information, providing a natural way to use unlabeled data.

In this work, we present new similarity measures to discover deeper relationship between q/a pairs based on a probabilistic model. We investigate two methods using Latent Dirichlet Allocation (LDA) (Blei, 2003) in § 3, and hierarchical LDA (hLDA) (Blei, 2009) in § 4 to discover hidden concepts. We present ways of utilizing this information within a discriminative classifier in § 5. With empirical experiments in § 6, we analyze the effects of generative model outcome on a QA system. With the new representation of conceptual structures on QA

Proceedings of the NAACL HLT 2010 Workshop on Semantic Search, pages 1–9,
Los Angeles, California, June 2010.

datasets, using a limited amount of world knowledge, we show performance improvements.

2 Background and Motivation

Previous research have focused on improving modules of the QA pipeline such as question processing (Huang et al., 2009), information retrieval (Clarke et al., 2006), information extraction (Saggion and Gaizauskas, 2006). Recent work on textual entailment has shown improvements on QA results (Harabagiu and Hickl, 2006), (Celikyilmaz et al., 2009), when used for filtering and ranking answers. They discover similarities between q/a pairs, where the answer to a question should be entailed by the text that supports the correctness of its answer.

In this paper, we present a ranking schema focusing on a new similarity modeling approach via generative and discriminative methods to utilize best features of both approaches. Combinations of discriminative and generative methodologies have been explored by several authors, e.g. (Bouchard and Triggs, 2004; McCallum et al., 2006; Bishop and Lasserre, 2007; Schmah et al., 2009), in many fields such as natural language processing, speech recognition, etc. In particular, the recent "deep learning" approaches (Weston et al., 2008) rely heavily on a hybrid generative-discriminative approach: an unsupervised generative learning phase followed by a discriminative fine-tuning.

In an analogical way to the deep learning methods, we discover relations between the q/a pairs based on the similarities on their *latent topics* discovered via Bayesian probabilistic approach. We investigate different ways of discovering topic based similarities following the fact that it is more likely that the candidate passage entails given question and contains true answer if they share similar topics. Later we combine this information in different ways into a discriminative classifier-based QA model.

The underlying mechanism of our similarity modeling approach is Latent Dirichlet Allocation (LDA) (Blei et al., 2003b). We argue that similarities can be characterized better if we define a semantic similarity measure based on hidden concepts (topics) on top of lexico-syntactic features. We later extend our similarity model using a hierarchical LDA (hLDA) (Blei et al., 2003a) to discover latent topics that are organized into hierarchies. A hierarchical structure is particularly appealing to QA task than a flat LDA, in that one can discover abstract and specific topics. For example, discovering that *baseball* and *football* are both contained in a more abstract class *sports* can help to relate to a general topic of a question.

3 Similarity Modeling with LDA

We assume that for a question posed by a user, the document sets D are retrieved by a search engine based on the query expanded from the question. Our aim is to build a measure to characterize similarities between a given question and each candidate passage/sentence $s \in D$ in the retrieved documents based on similarities of their hidden topics. Thus, we built bayesian probabilistic models on passage level rather than document level to *explicitly* extract their hidden topics. Moreover, the fact that there is limited amount of retrieved documents D per question ($\sim$100 documents) makes it appealing to build probabilistic models on passages in place of documents and define semantically coherent groups in passages as *latent concepts*. Given window size n sentences, we define a passage as $s = (|D| - n) + 1$ based on a n-sliding-window, where $|D|$ is the total number of sentences in retrieved documents D. There are 25+ sentences in documents, hence we extracted around 2500 passages for each question.

3.1 LDA Model for Q/A System

We briefly describe LDA (Blei et al., 2003b) model as used in our QA system. A passage in retrieved documents (document collection) is represented as a mixture of fixed topics, with topic z getting weight $\theta_z^{(s)}$ in passage s and each topic is a distribution over a finite vocabulary of words, with word w having a probability $\phi_w^{(z)}$ in topic z. Placing symmetric Dirichlet priors on $\theta^{(s)}$ and $\phi^{(z)}$, with $\theta^{(s)} \sim Dirichlet(\alpha)$ and $\phi^{(z)} \sim Dirichlet(\beta)$, where α and β are hyper-parameters to control the sparsity of distributions, the generative model is given by:

$$\begin{array}{lcll} w_i|z_i, \phi_{w_i}^{(z_i)} & \sim & Discrete(\phi^{(z_i)}), & i = 1, ..., W \\ \phi^{(z)} & \sim & Dirichlet(\beta), & z = 1, ..., K \\ z_i|\theta^{(s_i)} & \sim & Discrete(\theta^{(s_i)}), & i = 1, ..., W \\ \theta^{(s)} & \sim & Dirichlet(\alpha), & s = 1, ..., S \end{array} \quad (1)$$

where S is the number of passages discovered from the document collection, K is the total number of topics, W is the total number of words in the document collection, and s_i and z_i are the passage and the topic of the ith word w_i, respectively. Each word in the vocabulary $w_i \in V = \{w_1, ... w_W\}$ is assigned to each latent topic variable $z_{i=1,...,W}$ of words.

After seeing the data, our goal is to calculate the expected posterior probabilities $\hat{\phi}^{(z_i)}_{w_i}$ of a word w_i in a candidate passage given a topic $z_i = k$ and expected posterior probability $\hat{\theta}^{(s)}$ of topic mixings of a given passage s, using the count matrices:

$$\hat{\phi}^{(z_i)}_{w_i} = \frac{n^{WK}_{w_ik}+\beta}{\sum_{j=1}^{W} n^{WK}_{w_jk}+W\beta} \qquad \hat{\theta}^{(s)} = \frac{n^{SK}_{sk}+\alpha}{\sum_{j=1}^{K} n^{SK}_{sj}+K\alpha} \tag{2}$$

where $n^{WK}_{w_ik}$ is the count of w_i in topic k, and n^{SK}_{sk} is the count of topic k in passage s. The LDA model makes no attempt to account for the relation of topic mixtures, i.e., topics are distributed *flat*, and each passage is a distribution over all topics.

3.2 Degree of Similarity Between Q/A via Topics from LDA:

We build a LDA model on the set of retrieved passages s along with a given question q and calculate the *degree of similarity* DES^{LDA}(*q*,*s*) between each q/a pair based on two measures (Algorithm 1):

(1) $\boldsymbol{sim_1^{LDA}}$: To capture the lexical similarities on hidden topics, we represent each s and q as two probability distributions at each topic $z = k$. Thus, we sample sparse unigram distributions from each $\hat{\phi}^{(z)}$ using the words in q and s. Each sparse word given topic distribution is denoted as $p_q^{(z)} = p(\mathbf{w}_q|z, \hat{\phi}^{(z)})$ with the set of words $\mathbf{w}_q = (w_1, ..., w_{|q|})$ in q and $p_s = p(\mathbf{w}_s|z, \hat{\phi}^{(z)})$ with the set of words $\mathbf{w}_s = (w_1, ..., w_{|s|})$ in s, and $z = 1...K$ represent each topic.

The sparse probability distributions per topic are represented with only the words in q and s, and the probabilities of the rest of the words in V are set to zero. The W dimensional word probabilities is the expected posteriors obtained from LDA model (Eq.(2)), $p_s^{(z)} = (\hat{\phi}^{(z)}_{w_1}, ..., \hat{\phi}^{(z)}_{w_{|s|}}, 0, 0, ..) \in (0,1)^W$, $p_q^{(z)} = (\hat{\phi}^{(z)}_{w_1}, ..., \hat{\phi}^{(z)}_{w_{|q|}}, 0, 0, ..) \in (0,1)^W$. Given a topic z, the similarity between $p_q^{(z)}$ and $p_s^{(z)}$ is measured via transformed information radius (*IR*). We

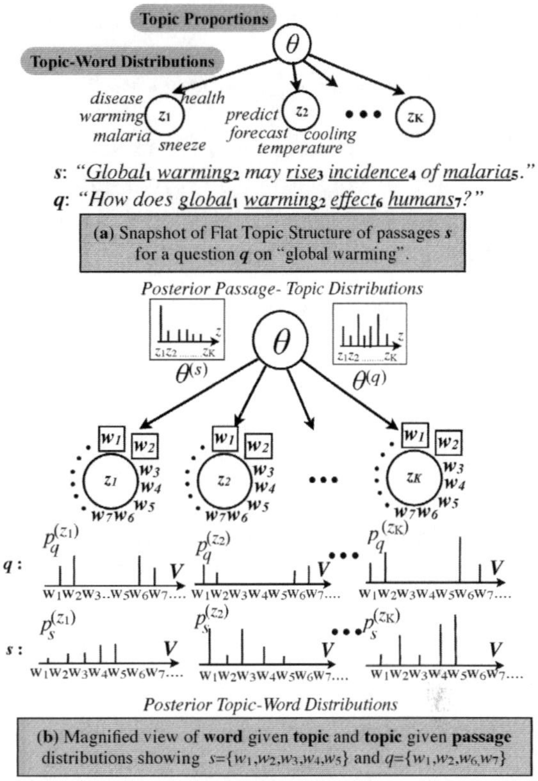

Figure 1: (a) The topic distributions of a passage s and a question q obtained from LDA. Each topic z_k is a distribution over words (Most probable terms are illustrated). (b) magnified view of (a) demonstrating sparse distributions over the vocabulary V, where only words in passage s and question q get values. The passage-topic distributions are topic mixtures, $\theta^{(s)}$ and $\theta^{(q)}$, for s and q.

first measure the divergence at each topic using *IR* based on Kullback-Liebler (*KL*) divergence:

$$IR(p_q^{(z)}, p_s^{(z)}) = KL(p_q^{(z)} || \tfrac{p_q^{(z)}+p_s^{(z)}}{2}) + KL(p_s^{(z)} || \tfrac{p_q^{(z)}+p_s^{(z)}}{2}) \tag{3}$$

where, $KL(p||q) = \sum_i p_i \log \frac{p_i}{q_i}$. The divergence is transformed into similarity measure (Manning and Schutze, 1999):

$$W(p_q^{(z)}, p_s^{(z)}) = 10^{-\delta IR(p_q^{(z)}, p_s^{(z)})} \text{[1]} \tag{4}$$

To measure the similarity between probability distributions we opted for *IR* instead of commonly used *KL* because with *IR* there is no problem with infinite values since $\frac{p_q+p_s}{2} \neq 0$ if either $p_q \neq 0$ or $p_s \neq 0$, and it is also symmetric, *IR(p,q)*=*IR(q,p)*. The similarity of q/a pairs on topic-word basis is the average

[1] In experiments $\delta = 1$ is used.

of transformed divergence over the entire K topics:

$$sim_1^{LDA}(q,s) = \frac{1}{K}\sum_{k=1}^{K} W(p_q^{(z=k)}, p_s^{(z=k)}) \quad (5)$$

(2) sim_2^{LDA}: We introduce another measure based on passage-topic mixing proportions in q and s to capture similarities between their topics using the transformed *IR* in Eq.(4) as follows:

$$sim_2^{LDA}(q,s) = 10^{-IR(\hat{\theta}^{(q)},\hat{\theta}^{(s)})} \quad (6)$$

The $\hat{\theta}^{(q)}$ and $\hat{\theta}^{(s)}$ are K-dimensional discrete topic weights in question q and a passage s from Eq.(2). In summary, sim_1^{LDA} is a measure of lexical similarity on topic-word level and sim_2^{LDA} is a measure of topical similarity on passage level. Together they form the *degree of similarity* $DES^{LDA}(s,q)$ and are combined as follows:

$$DES^{LDA}(s,q) = sim_1^{LDA}(q,s) * sim_2^{LDA}(q,s) \quad (7)$$

Fig.1 shows sparse distributions obtained for sample q and s. Since the topics are not distributed hierarchially, each topic distribution is over the entire vocabulary of words in retrieved collection D. Fig.1 only shows the most probable words in a given topic. Moreover, each s and q are represented as a discrete probability distribution over all K topics.

Algorithm 1 Flat Topic-Based Similarity Model

Given a query q and candidate passages $s \in D$
Build an LDA model for the retrieved passages.
for each passages $s \in D$ **do**
  - Calculate $sim_1(q,s)$ using Eq.(5)
  - Calculate $sim_2(q,s)$ using Eq.(6)
  - Calculate degree of similarity between q and s:
    $DES^{LDA}(q,s) = sim_1(q,s) * sim_2(q,s)$
end for

4 Similarity Modeling with hLDA

Given a question, we discover hidden topic distributions using hLDA (Blei et al., 2003a). hLDA organizes topics into a tree of a fixed depth L (Fig.2.(a)), as opposed to *flat* LDA. Each candidate passage s is assigned to a path c_s in the topic tree and each word w_i in s is assigned to a hidden topic z_s at a level l of c_s. Each node is associated with a topic distribution over words. The Gibbs sampler (Griffiths and Steyvers, 2004) alternates between choosing a new path for each passage through the tree and assigning each word in each passage to a topic along that path. The structure of tree is learnt along with the topics using a nested Chinese restaurant process (nCRP) (Blei et al., 2003a), which is used as a prior.

The nCRP is a stochastic process, which assigns probability distributions to infinitely branching and deep trees. nCRP specifies a distribution of words in passages into paths in an L-level tree. Assignments of passages to paths are sampled sequentially: The first passage takes the initial L-level path, starting with a single branch tree. Next, mth subsequent passage is assigned to a path drawn from distribution:

$$\begin{aligned} p(path_{old}, c|m, m_c) &= \frac{m_c}{\gamma+m-1} \\ p(path_{new}, c|m, m_c) &= \frac{\gamma}{\gamma+m-1} \end{aligned} \quad (8)$$

$path_{old}$ and $path_{new}$ represent an existing and novel (branch) path consecutively, m_c is the number of previous passages assigned to path c, m is the total number of passages seen so far, and γ is a hyper-parameter, which controls the probability of creating new paths. Based on this probability each node can branch out a different number of child nodes proportional to γ. The generative process for hLDA is:

(1) For each topic $k \in T$, sample a distribution $\beta_k \backsim$ Dirichlet(η).

(2) For each passage s in retrieved documents,

  (a) Draw a path $c_s \backsim$ nCRP(γ),

  (b) Sample L-vector θ_s mixing weights from Dirichlet distribution $\theta_s \sim Dir(\alpha)$.

  (c) For each word n, choose :

    (*i*) a level $z_{s,n}|\theta_s$, (*ii*) a word $w_{s,n}|\{z_{s,n}, c_s, \beta\}$

Given passage s, θ_s is a vector of topic proportions from L dimensional Dirichlet parameterized by α (distribution over levels in the tree.) The nth word of s is sampled by first choosing a level $z_{s,n} = l$ from the discrete distribution θ_s with probability $\theta_{s,l}$. Dirichlet parameter η and γ control the size of tree effecting the number of topics. Large values of η favor more topics (Blei et al., 2003a).

Model Learning: Gibbs sampling is a common method to fit the hLDA models. The aim is to obtain the following samples from the posterior of: (*i*) the latent tree T, (*ii*) the level assignment **z** for all words, (*iii*) the path assignments **c** for all passages conditioned on the observed words **w**.

Given the assignment of words **w** to levels **z** and assignments of passages to paths **c**, the expected

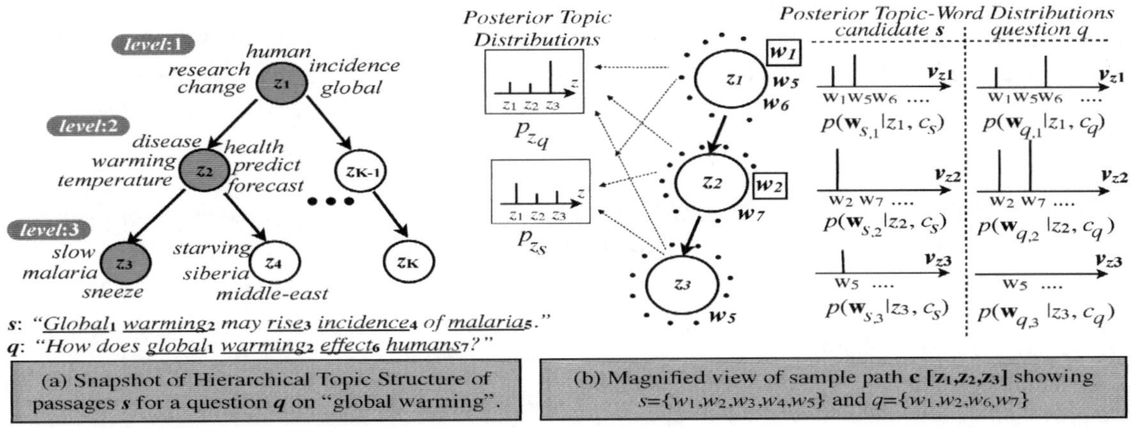

Figure 2: (a) A sample 3-level tree using hLDA. Each passage is associated with a path c through the hierarchy, where each node $z_s = l$ is associated with a distribution over terms (Most probable terms are illustrated). (b) magnified view of a path (darker nodes) in (a). Distribution of words in given passage s and a question (q) using sub-vocabulary of words at each level topic v_l. Discrete distributions on the left are topic mixtures for each passage, p_{z_q} and p_{z_s}.

posterior probability of a particular word w at a given topic **z**=l of a path **c**=c is proportional to the number of times w was generated by that topic:

$$p(w|\mathbf{z}, \mathbf{c}, \mathbf{w}, \eta) \propto n_{(\mathbf{z}=l, \mathbf{c}=c, \mathbf{w}=w)} + \eta \quad (9)$$

Similarly, posterior probability of a particular topic z in a given passage s is proportional to number of times z was generated by that passage:

$$p(z|s, \mathbf{z}, \mathbf{c}, \alpha) \propto n_{(\mathbf{c}=c_c, \mathbf{z}=l)} + \alpha \quad (10)$$

$n_{(.)}$ is the count of elements of an array satisfying the condition. Posterior probabilities are normalized with total counts and their hyperparameters.

4.1 Tree-Based Similarity Model

The hLDA constructs a hierarchical tree structure of candidate passages and given question, each of which are represented by a path in the tree, and each path can be shared by many passages/question. The assumption is that passages sharing the same path should be more similar to each other because they share the same topics (Fig.2). Moreover, if a path includes a question, then other passages on that path are more likely to entail the question than passages on the other paths. Thus, the similarity of a candidate passage s to a question q sharing the same path is a measure of semantic similarity (Algorithm 2). Given a question, we build an hLDA model on retrieved passages. Let c_q be the path for a given q. We identify the candidate passages that share the same path with q, $M = \{s \in D | c_s = c_q\}$. Given path c_q and M, we calculate the degree of similarity $DES^{hLDA}(s, q)$ between q and s by calculating two similarity measures:

(1) sim_1^{hLDA}: We define two sparse (discrete) unigram distributions for candidate s and question q at each node l to define lexical similarities on topic level. The distributions are over a vocabulary of words generated by the topic at that node, $v_l \subset V$. Note that, in hLDA the topic distributions at each level of a path is sampled from the vocabulary of passages sharing that path, contrary to LDA, in which the topics are over entire vocabulary of words. This enables defining a similarity measure on specific topics. Given $\mathbf{w}_q = \{w_1, ..., w_{|q|}\}$, let $\mathbf{w}_{q,l} \subset \mathbf{w}_q$ be the set of words in q that are generated from topic $\mathbf{z}_q$ at level l on path c_q. The discrete unigram distribution $p_{ql} = p(\mathbf{w}_{q,l}|\mathbf{z}_q = l, c_q, v_l)$ represents the probability over all words v_l assigned to topic $\mathbf{z}_q$ at level l, by sampling only for words in $\mathbf{w}_{q,l}$. The probability of the rest of the words in v_l are set 0. Similarly, $p_{s,l} = p(\mathbf{w}_{s,l}|\mathbf{z}_s, c_q, v_l)$ is the probability of words $\mathbf{w}_s$ in s extracted from the same topic (see Fig.2.b). The word probabilities in $p_{q,l}$ and $p_{s,l}$ are obtained using Eq. (9) and then normalized.

The similarity between $p_{q,l}$ and $p_{s,l}$ at each level is obtained by transformed information radius:

$$W_{c_{q,l}}(p_{q,l}, p_{s,l}) = 10^{\delta\text{-}IR_{c_{q,l}}(p_{q,l}, p_{s,l})} \quad (11)$$

where the $IR_{c_{q,l}}(p_{q,l}, p_{s,l})$ is calculated as in Eq.(3) this time for $p_{q,l}$ and $p_{s,l}$ ($\delta = 1$). Finally sim_1^{hLDA} is obtained by averaging Eq.(11) over different levels:

$$sim_1^{hLDA}(q,s) = \frac{1}{L}\sum_{l=1}^{L} W_{c_q,l}(p_{q,l}, p_{s,l}) * l \quad (12)$$

The similarity between $p_{q,l}$ and $p_{s,l}$ is weighted by the level l because the similarity should be rewarded if there is a specific word overlap at child nodes.

Algorithm 2 Tree-Based Similarity Model

1: Given candidate passages s and question q.
2: Build hLDA on set of s and q to obtain tree T.
3: Find path c_q on tree T and candidate passages
4: on path c_q, i.e., $M = \{s \in D | c_s = c_q\}$.
5: **for** candidate passage $s \in M$ **do**
6: Find $DES^{hDLA}(q,s) = sim_1^{hLDA} * sim_2^{hLDA}$
7: using Eq.(12) and Eq.(13)
8: **end for**
9: **if** $s \notin M$, **then** $DES^{hDLA}(q,s)$=0.

(2) sim_2^{hLDA}: We introduce a concept-base measure based on passage-topic mixing proportions to calculate the topical similarities between q and s. We calculate the topic proportions of q and s, represented by $p_{z_q} = p(\mathbf{z}_q|c_q)$ and $p_{z_s} = p(\mathbf{z}_s|c_q)$ via Eq.(10). The similarity between the distributions is then measured with transformed IR as in Eq.(11) by:

$$sim_2^{hLDA}(q,s) = 10^{-IR_{c_q}(p_{z_q}, p_{z_s})} \quad (13)$$

In summary, sim_1^{hLDA} provides information about the similarity between q and s based on topic-word distributions, and sim_2^{hLDA} is the similarity between the weights of their topics. The two measures are combined to calculate the degree of similarity:

$$DES^{hLDA}(q,s) = sim_1^{hLDA}(q,s) * sim_2^{hLDA}(q,s) \quad (14)$$

Fig.2.b depicts a sample path illustrating sparse unigram distributions of a q and s at each level and their topic proportions, p_{z_q}, and p_{z_s}. The candidate passages that are not on the same path as the question are assigned $DES^{hLDA}(s,q) = 0$.

5 Discriminitive Model for QA

In (Celikyilmaz et al., 2009), the QA task is posed as a textual entailment problem using lexical and semantic features to characterize similarities between q/a pairs. A discriminative classifier is built to predict the existence of an answer in candidate sentences. Although they show that semi-supervised methods improve accuracy of their QA model under limited amount of labeled data, they suggest that with sufficient number of labeled data, supervised methods outperform semi-supervised methods. We argue that there is a lot to discover from unlabeled text to help improve QA accuracy. Thus, we propose using Bayesian probabilistic models. First we briefly present the baseline method:

`Baseline:` We use the supervised classifier model presented in (Celikyilmaz et al., 2009) as our baseline QA model. Their datasets, provided in http://www.eecs.berkeley.edu/~asli/asliPublish.html, are q/a pairs from TREC task. They define each q/a pair as a d dimensional feature vector $x_i \in \Re^d$ characterizing entailment information between them. They build a support vector machine (SVM) (Drucker et al., 1997) classifier model to predict the entailment scores for q/a pairs.

To characterize the similarity between q/a pairs they use: (*i*) features represented by similarities between semantic components, e.g., subject, object, verb, or named-entity types discovered in q/a pairs, and (*ii*) lexical features represented by lexico-syntactic alignments such as n-gram word overlaps or cause and entailment relations discovered from WordNet (Miller, 1995). For a given question q, they rank the candidate sentences s based on predicted entailment scores from the classifier, $TE(q,s)$.

We extend the baseline by using the degree of similarity between question and candidate passage obtained from LDA, $DES^{LDA}(q,s)$, as well as hLDA $DES^{hLDA}(q,s)$, and evaluate different models:

`Model M-1:` Degree of Similarity as Rank Scores: In this model, the QA is based on a fully generative approach in which the similarity measures of Eq.(7) in §3 and Eq.(14) in §4 are used to obtain ranking scores. We build two separate models, `M-1.1` using $DES^{LDA}(q,s)$, and `M-1.2` using $DES^{hLDA}(q,s)$ as rank scores and measure accuracy by re-ranking candidate passages accordingly. Given a question, this model requires training individual LDA and hLDA models.

`Model M-2:` Interpolation Between Classifier-Based Entailment Scores and Generative Model Scores: In this model, the underlying mechanism of QA is the discriminative method presented in baseline. We linearly combine the probabilistic similarity scores from generative models, *DES* scores in `M-1`, with the baseline scores. We build two additional models to calculate the final rank scores; `M-2.1` using:

$$score(s|q) = a{*}TE(q,s){+}b{*}DES^{LDA}(q,s) \quad (15)$$

and `M-2.2` using:

$$score(s|q) = a{*}TE(q,s){+}b{*}DES^{hLDA}(q,s) \quad (16)$$

where $0 \leq a \leq 1$ and $0 \leq b \leq 1$ and $a + b = 1$. We find the optimum a^* and b^* based on the validation experiments on training dataset. The candidate sentences are re-ranked based on these scores.

`Model M-3`: Degree of Similarity as Entailment Features: Another way to incorporate the latent information into the discriminitive QA model is to utilize the latent similarities as explanatory variables in the classifier model. Particularly we build `M-3.1` by using sim_1^{LDA}, sim_2^{LDA} as well as $DES^{LDA}(q,s)$ as additional features for the SVM, on top of the the existing features used in (Celikyilmaz et al., 2009). Similarly, we build `M-3.2` by using sim_1^{hLDA}, sim_2^{hLDA} as well as $DES^{hLDA}(q,s)$ as additional features to the SVM classifier model to predict entailment scores. This model requires building two new SVM classifier models with the new features.

6 Experiments and Discussions

We demonstrate the results of our experiments on exploration of the effect of different generative models presented in §5 on TREC QA datasets.

We performed experiments on the datasets used in (Celikyilmaz et al., 2009). Their train dataset composes of a set of 1449 questions from TREC-99-03. For each question, the 5 top-ranked candidate sentences are extracted from a large newswire corpora (Acquaint corpus) through a search engine, i.e., Lucene [2]. The q/a pairs are labeled as true/false depending on the containment of the true answer string in retrieved passages. Additionally, to calculate the LDA and hLDA similarity measures for each candidate passage, we also extract around 100 documents in the same fashion using Lucene and identify passages to build the probabilistic models. We calculate the probabilistic similarities, i.e., sim_1^{LDA}, sim_2^{LDA}, sim_1^{hLDA}, sim_2^{hLDA}, and the degree of similarity values, i.e., $DES^{LDA}(q,s)$ and $DES^{hLDA}(q,s)$ for each of the 5 top-ranked candidate sentences in training dataset at inference time. Around 7200 q/a pairs are compiled accordingly.

The provided testing data contains a set of 202 questions from TREC2004 along with 20 candidate sentences for each question, which are labeled as true/false. To calculate the similarities for the 20 candidate sentences, we extract around 100 documents for each question and build LDA and hLDA models. 4037 testing q/a pairs are compiled.

We report the retrieval performance of our models in terms of Mean Reciprocal Rank (MRR), top 1 (Top1) and top 5 prediction accuracies (Top5) (Voorhees, 2004). We performed parameter optimization during training based on prediction accuracy to find the best $C = \{10^{-2}, .., 10^{2}\}$ and $\Gamma = \{2^{-2}, .., 2^{3}\}$ for RBF kernel SVM. For the LDA models we present the results with 10 topics. In hLDA models, we use four levels for the tree construction and set the topic Dirichlet hyperparameters in decreasing order of levels at $\eta = \{1.0, 0.75, 0.5, 0.25\}$ to encourage as many terms in the mid to low levels as the higher levels in the hierarchy, for a better comparison between q/a pairs. The nested CRP parameter γ is fixed at 1.0. We evaluated n-sliding-window size of sentences in sequence, $n = \{1, 3, 5\}$, to compile candidate passages for probabilistic models (Table 1). The output scores for SVM models are normalized to [0,1].

⋆ As our baseline (in §5), we consider supervised classifier based QA presented in (Celikyilmaz et al., 2009). The baseline MRR on TREC-2004 dataset is MRR=%67.6, Top1=%58, Top5=%82.2.

⋆ The results of the new models on testing dataset are reported in Table 1. Incorporating the generative model output to the classifier model as input features, i.e., `M-3.1` and `M-3-2`, performs consistently better than the rest of the models and the baseline, where MRR result is statistically significant based on t-test statistics (at $p = 0.95$ confidence level). When combined with the textual entailment scores, i.e., `M-2.1` and `M-2.2`, they provide a slightly better ranking, a minor improvement compared to the baseline. However, using the generative model outcome as sole ranking scores in

[2] http://lucene.apache.org/java/

	Window-size	1-window			3-window			5-window		
	MRR categories	MRR	Top1	Top5	MRR	Top1	Top5	MRR	Top1	Top5
Models	M-1.1 (with LDA)	42.7	30.2	64.4	42.1	30.2	64.4	42.1	30.2	64.4
	M-1.1 (with hLDA)	55.8	45.5	71.0	55.8	45.5	71.0	54.9	45.5	71.0
	M-2.1 (with LDA)	66.2	55.1	82.2	65.2	54.5	80.7	65.2	54.5	80.7
	M-2.2 (with hLDA)	68.2	58.4	82.2	67.6	58.0	82.2	67.4	58.0	81.6
	M-3.1 (with LDA)	68.0	61.0	82.2	68.0	58.1	82.2	68.2	58.1	82.2
	M-3.2 (with hLDA)	68.4	**63.4**	82.2	68.3	**61.0**	82.2	68.3	**61.0**	82.2

Table 1: The MRR results of the models presented in §5 on testing dataset (TREC 2004) using different window sizes of candidate passages. The statistically significant model results in each corresponding MRR category are bolded. Baseline MRR=%67.6, Top1=%58, Top5=%82.2.

M-1.1 and M-1.2 do not reveal as good results as the other models, suggesting room for improvement.

⋆ In Table 1, Top1 MRR yields better improvement compared to the other two MRRs, especially for models M-3.1 and M-3.2. This suggests that the probabilistic model outcome rewards the candidate sentences containing the true answer by estimating higher scores and moves them up to the higher levels of the rank.

⋆ The analysis of different passage sizes suggest that the 1-window size yields best results and no significant performance improvement is observed when window size is increased. Thus, the similarity between q/a pairs can be better explained if the candidate passage contains less redundant sentences.

⋆ The fact that the similarity scores obtained from the hLDA models are significantly better than LDA models in Table 1 indicates an important property of hierarchal topic models. With the hLDA specific and generic topics can be identified on different levels of the hierarchy. Two candidate passages can be characterized with different abstract and specific topics (Fig. 2) enabling representation of better features to identify similarity measures between them. Whereas in LDA, each candidate passage has a proportion in each topic. Rewarding the similarities on specific topics with the hLDA models help improve the QA rank performance.

⋆ In M-3.1 and M-3.2 we use probabilistic similarities and *DES* as inputs to the classifier. In Table 2 we show the individual effects of these features on the MRR testing performance along with other lexical and semantic features of the baseline. Although the effect of each feature is comparable, the DES^{LDA} and DES^{hLDA} features reveal slightly better results.

Features	M-3.1	Features	M-3.1
$sim1^{LDA}$	67.7	$sim1^{hLDA}$	67.8
$sim2^{LDA}$	67.5	$sim2^{hLDA}$	68.0
DES^{LDA}	67.9	DES^{hLDA}	68.1

Table 2: The MRR results of the similarity measures on testing dataset (TREC 2004) when used as input features.

7 Conclusion and Future Work

In this paper we introduced a set of methods based on Latent Dirichlet Allocation (LDA) to characterize the similarity between the question and the candidate passages, which are used as ranking scores. The results of our experiments suggest that extracting information from hidden concepts improves the results of a classifier-based QA model.

Although unlabeled data exploration through probabilistic graphical models can help to improve information extraction, devising a machinery with suitable generative models for the given natural language task is a challenge. This work helps with such understanding via extensive simulations and puts forward and confirms a hypothesis explaining the mechanisms behind the effect of unsupervised pre-training for the final discriminant learning task.

In the future, we would like to further evaluate the models presented in this paper for larger datasets and for different tasks such as question paraphrase retrieval or query expansion. Moreover, we would like to enhance the similarities with other semantic components extracted from questions such as question topic and question focus.

References

C. M. Bishop and J. Lasserre. Generative or discriminative? getting the best of both worlds. In *In Bayesian Statistics 8, Bernardo, J. M. et al. (Eds), Oxford University Press*, 2007.

D. Blei, T. Griffiths, M. Jordan, and J. Tenenbaum. Hierarchical topic models and the nested chinese restaurant process. In *In Neural Information Processing Systems [NIPS]*, 2003a.

D. M. Blei, A. Ng, and M. Jordan. Latent dirichlet allocation. In *Jrnl. Machine Learning Research, 3:993-1022*, 2003b.

G. Bouchard and B. Triggs. The tradeoff between generative and discriminative classifiers. In *Proc. of COMPSTAT'04*, 2004.

A. Celikyilmaz, M. Thint, and Z. Huang. Graph-based semi-supervised learning for question answering. In *Proc. of the ACL-2009*, 2009.

C.L.A. Clarke, G. V. Cormack, R. T. Lynam, and E. L. Terra. Question answering by passage selection. In *In: Advances in open domain question answering, Strzalkowski, and Harabagiu (Eds.)*, pages 259–283. Springer, 2006.

H. Drucker, C.J.C. Burger, L. Kaufman, A. Smola, and V. Vapnik. Support vector regression machines. In *NIPS 9*, 1997.

A. Echihabi and D. Marcu. A noisy-channel approach to question answering. In *ACL-2003*, 2003.

T. Griffiths and M. Steyvers. Finding scientific topics. In *PNAS, 101(Supp. 1): 5228-5235*, 2004.

S. Harabagiu and A. Hickl. Methods for using textual entailment in open-domain question answering. In *In Proc. of ACL-2006*, pages 905–912, 2006.

Z. Huang, M. Thint, and A. Celikyilmaz. Investigation of question classifier in question answering. In *In EMNLP'09*, 2009.

W.-Y. Ma and K. McKeowon. Where's the verb? correcting machine translation during question answering. In *In ACL-IJCNLP'09*, 2009.

C. Manning and H. Schutze. Foundations of statistical natural language processing. In *MIT Press. Cambridge, MA*, 1999.

A. McCallum, C. Pal, G. Druck, and X. Wang. Multi-conditional learning: Generative/discriminative training for clustering and classification. In *AAAI 2006*, 2006.

G.A. Miller. Wordnet: A lexical database for english. In *ACM*, 1995.

D. Molla, M.V. Zaanen, and D. Smith. Named entity recognition for question answering. In *In ALTW2006*, 2006.

H.T. Ng, J.L.P. Kwan, and Y. Xia. Question answering using a large text database: A machine learning approach. In *EMNLP-2001*, 2001.

H. Saggion and R. Gaizauskas. Experiments in passage selection and answer extraction for question answering. In *In: Advances in open domain question answering, Strzalkowski, and Harabagiu (Eds.)*, pages 291–302. Springer, 2006.

T. Schmah, G. E Hinton, R. Zemel, S. L. Small, and S. Strother. Generative versus discriminative training of rbms for classification of fmri images. In *Proc. NIPS 2009*, 2009.

Dan Shen and Dietrich Klakow. Exploring correlation of dependency relation paths for answer extraction. In *Proc. of ACL-2006*, 2006.

J.L. Vicedo and A. Ferrandez. Applying anaphora resolution to question answering and information retrieval systems. In *In LNCS*, volume 1846, pages 344–355, 2000.

Ellen M. Voorhees. Overview of trec2004 question answering track. 2004.

J. Weston, F. Rattle, and R. Collobert. Deep learning via semi-supervised embedding. In *ICML*, 2008.

Experts' Retrieval with Multiword-Enhanced Author Topic Model

Nikhil Johri Dan Roth **Yuancheng Tu**
Dept. of Computer Science Dept. of Linguistics
University of Illinois at Urbana-Champaign
{njohri2,danr,ytu}@illinois.edu

Abstract

In this paper, we propose a multiword-enhanced author topic model that clusters authors with similar interests and expertise, and apply it to an information retrieval system that returns a ranked list of authors related to a keyword. For example, we can retrieve *Eugene Charniak* via search for *statistical parsing*.

The existing works on author topic modeling assume a "bag-of-words" representation. However, many semantic atomic concepts are represented by multiwords in text documents. This paper presents a pre-computation step as a way to discover these multiwords in the corpus automatically and tags them in the term-document matrix. The key advantage of this method is that it retains the simplicity and the computational efficiency of the unigram model. In addition to a qualitative evaluation, we evaluate the results by using the topic models as a component in a search engine. We exhibit improved retrieval scores when the documents are represented via sets of latent topics and authors.

1 Introduction

This paper addresses the problem of searching people with similar interests and expertise without inputting personal names as queries. Many existing people search engines need people's names to do a "keyword" style search, using a person's name as a query. However, in many situations, such information is impossible to know beforehand. Imagine a scenario where the statistics department of a university invited a world-wide known expert in Bayesian statistics and machine learning to give a keynote speech; how can the department head notify all the people on campus who are interested without spamming those who are not? Our paper proposes a solution to the aforementioned scenario by providing a search engine which goes beyond "keyword" search and can retrieve such information semantically. The department head would only need to input the domain keyword of the keynote speaker, i.e. *Bayesian statistics, machine learning*, and all professors and students who are interested in this topic will be retrieved. Specifically, we propose a **M**ultiword-enhanced **A**uthor-**T**opic **M**odel (MATM), a probabilistic generative model which assumes two steps of generation process when producing a document.

Statistical topical modeling (Blei and Lafferty, 2009a) has attracted much attention recently due to its broad applications in machine learning, text mining and information retrieval. In these models, semantic topics are represented by multinomial distribution over words. Typically, the content of each topic is visualized by simply listing the words in order of decreasing probability and the "meaning" of each topic is reflected by the top 10 to 20 words in that list. The Author-Topic Model (ATM) (Steyvers et al., 2004; Rosen-Zvi et al., 2004) extends the basic topical models to include author information in which topics and authors are modeled jointly. Each author is a multinomial distribution over topics and each topic is a multinomial distribution over words.

Our contribution to this paper is two-fold. First of all, our model, MATM, extends the original ATM by adding semantically coherent multiwords into the term-document matrix to relax the model's "bag-of-

Proceedings of the NAACL HLT 2010 Workshop on Semantic Search, pages 10–18,
Los Angeles, California, June 2010.

words" assumption. Each multiword is discovered via statistical measurement and filtered by its part of speech pattern via an off-line way. One key advantage of tagging these semantic atomic units off-line, is the retention of the flexibility and computational efficiency in using the simpler word exchangeable model, while providing better interpretation of the topics author distribution.

Secondly, to the best of our knowledge, this is the first proposal to apply the enhanced author topic modeling in a semantic retrieval scenario, where searching people is associated with a set of hidden semantically meaningful topics instead of their names. While current search engines cannot support interactive and exploratory search effectively, search based on our model serves very well to answer a range of exploratory queries about the document collections by semantically linking the interests of the authors to the topics of the collection, and ultimately to the distribution of the words in the documents.

The rest of the paper is organized as follows. We present some related work on topic modeling, the original author-topic model and automatic phrase discovery methods in Sec. 2. Then our model is described in Sec. 3. Sec. 4 presents our experiments and the evaluation of our method on expert search. We conclude this paper in Sec. 5 with some discussion and several further developments.

2 Related Work

Author topic modeling, originally proposed in (Steyvers et al., 2004; Rosen-Zvi et al., 2004), is an extension of another popular topic model, Latent Dirichlet Allocation (LDA) (Blei et al., 2003), a probabilistic generative model that can be used to estimate the properties of multinomial observations via unsupervised learning. LDA represents each document as a mixture of probabilistic topics and each topic as a multinomial distribution over words. The Author topic model adds an author layer over LDA and assumes that the topic proportion of a given document is generated by the chosen author.

Both LDA and the author topic model assume *bag-of-words* representation. As shown by many previous works (Blei et al., 2003; Steyvers et al., 2004), even such unrealistic assumption can actually lead to a reasonable topic distribution with relatively simple and computationally efficient inference algorithm. However, this unigram representation also poses major handicap when interpreting and applying the hidden topic distributions. The proposed MATM is an effort to try to leverage this problem in author topic modeling. There have been some works on Ngram topic modeling over the original LDA model (Wallach, 2006; Wang and McCallum, 2005; Wang et al., 2007; Griffiths et al., 2007). However, to the best of our knowledge, this paper is the first to embed multiword expressions into the author topic model.

Many of these Ngram topic models (Wang and McCallum, 2005; Wang et al., 2007; Griffiths et al., 2007) improves the base model by adding a new indicator variable x_i to signify if a bigram should be generated. If $x_i = 1$, the word w_i is generated from a distribution that depends only on the previous word to form an Ngram. Otherwise, it is generated from a distribution only on the topic proportion (Griffiths et al., 2007) or both the previous words and the latent topic (Wang and McCallum, 2005; Wang et al., 2007). However, these complex models not only increase the parameter size to $\mathcal{V}$ times larger than the size of the original LDA model parameters ($\mathcal{V}$ is the size of the vocabulary of the document collection) [1], it also faces the problem of choosing which word to be the topic of the potential Ngram. In many text retrieval tasks, the humongous size of data may prevent us using such complicated computation on-line. However, our model retains the computational efficiency by adding a simple tagging process via pre-computation.

Another effort in the current literature to interpret the meaning of the topics is to label the topics via a post-processing way (Mei et al., 2007; Blei and Lafferty, 2009b; Magatti et al., 2009). For example, Probabilistic topic labeling (Mei et al., 2007) first extracts a set of candidate label phrases from a reference collection and represents each candidate labeling phrase with a multinomial distribution of words. Then KL divergence is used to rank the most probable labels for a given topic. This method needs not only extra reference text collection, but also facing

[1] LDA collocation models and topic Ngram models also have parameters for the binomial distribution of the indicator variable x_i for each word in the vocabulary.

the problem of finding discriminative and high coverage candidate labels. Blei and Lafferty (Blei and Lafferty, 2009b) proposed a method to annotate each word of the corpus by its posterior word topic distribution and then cast a statistical co-occurrence analysis to extract the most significant Ngrams for each topic and visualize the topic with these Ngrams. However, they only applied their method to basic LDA model.

In this paper, we applied our multiword extension to the author topic modeling and no extra reference corpora are needed. The MATM, with an extra pre-computing step to add meaningful multiwords into the term-document matrix, enables us to retain the flexibility and computational efficiency to use the simpler word exchangeable model, while providing better interpretation of the topics and author distribution.

3 Multiword-enhanced Author-Topic Model

The MATM is an extension of the original ATM (Rosen-Zvi et al., 2004; Steyvers et al., 2004) by semantically tagging collocations or multiword expressions, which represent atomic concepts in documents in the term-document matrix of the model. Such tagging procedure enables us to retain computational efficiency of the word-level exchangeability of the orginal ATM while provides more sensible topic distributions and better author topic coherence. The details of our model are presented in Algorithm 1.

3.1 Beyond Bag-of-Words Tagging

The first *for* loop in Algorithm 1 is the procedure of our multiword tagging. Commonly used ngrams, or statistically short phrases in text retrieval, or so-called collocations in natural language processing have long been studied by linguistics in various ways. Traditional collocation discovery methods range from frequency to mean and variance, from statistical hypothesis testing, to mutual information (Manning and Schtze, 1999). In this paper, we use a simple statistical hypothesis testing method, namely Pearson's chi-square test implemented in Ngram Statistic Package (Banerjee and Pedersen, 2003), enhanced by passing the candidate phrases through some pre-defined part of speech patterns that are likely to be true phrases. This very simple heuristic has been shown to improve the counting based methods significantly (Justenson and Katz, 1995).

The χ^2 test is chosen since it does not assume any normally distributed probabilities and the essence of this test is to compare the observed frequencies with the frequencies expected for independence. We choose this simple statistic method since in many text retrieval tasks the volume of data we see always makes it impractical to use very sophisticated statistical computations. We also focus on nominal phrases, such as bigram and trigram noun phrases since they are most likely to function as semantic atomic unit to directly represent the concepts in text documents.

3.2 Author Topic Modeling

The last three generative procedures described in Algorithm 1 jointly model the author and topic information. This generative model is adapted directly from (Steyvers et al., 2004). Graphically, it can be visualized as shown in Figure 1.

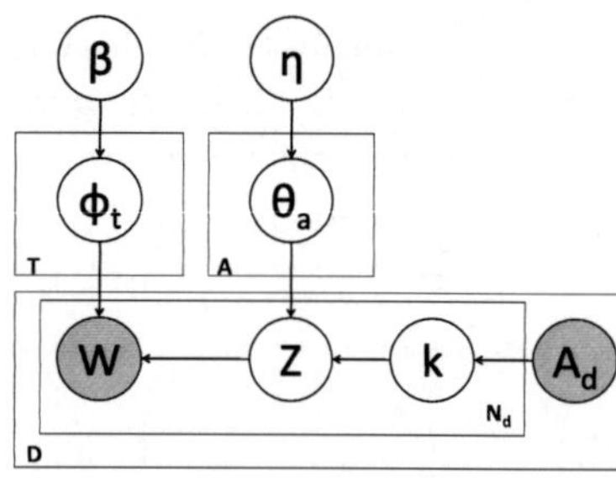

Figure 1: Plate notation of our model: MATM

The four plates in Fiture 1 represent topic (T), author (A), document (D) and Words in each document (N_d) respectively. Each author is associated with a multinomial distribution over all topics, $\vec{\theta_a}$ and each topic is a multinomial distribution over all words, $\vec{\phi_t}$. Each of these distribution has a symmetric Dirichlet prior over it, $\vec{\eta}$ and $\vec{\beta}$ respectively. When generating a document, an author *k* is first chosen according to a uniform distribution. Then this author chooses the topic from his/her associated multinomial distribution over topics and then generates a word from the multinomial distribution of that topic over the words.

Algorithm 1: MATM: $\mathcal{A}, \mathcal{T}, \mathcal{D}, \mathcal{N}$ are four plates as shown in Fig. 1. The first *for* loop is the off-line process of multiword expressions. The rest of the algorithm is the generative process of the author topic modeling.

Data: $\mathcal{A}, \mathcal{T}, \mathcal{D}, \mathcal{N}$

for *all documents* $d \in \mathcal{D}$ **do**
- Part-of-Speech tagging ;
- Bigram extraction ;
- Part-of Speech Pattern Filtering ;
- Add discovered bigrams into $\mathcal{N}$;

for *each author* $a \in \mathcal{A}$ **do**
- draw a distribution over topics: $\vec{\theta_a} \sim Dir_{\mathcal{T}}(\vec{\eta})$;

for *each topic* $t \in \mathcal{T}$ **do**
- draw a distribution over words: $\vec{\phi_t} \sim Dir_{\mathcal{N}}(\vec{\beta})$;

for *each document* $d \in \mathcal{D}$ *and* k *authors* $\in d$ **do**
- **for** *each word* $w \in d$ **do**
  - choose an author $k \sim$ uniformly;
  - draw a topic assignment i given the author: $z_{k,i}|k \sim Multinomial(\theta_a)$;
  - draw a word from the chosen topic: $w_{d,k,i}|z_{k,i} \sim Multinomial(\phi_{z_{k,i}})$;

MATM includes two sets of parameters. The $\mathcal{T}$ topic distribution over words, ϕ_t which is similar to that in LDA. However, instead of a document-topic distribution, author topic modeling has the author-topic distribution, θ_a. Using a matrix factorization interpretation, similar to what Steyvers, Griffiths and Hofmann have pointed out for LDA (Steyvers and Griffiths, 2007) and PLSI (Hofmann, 1999), a word-author co-occurrence matrix in author topic model can be split into two parts: a word-topic matrix ϕ and a topic-author matrix θ. And the hidden topic serves as the low dimensional representation for the content of the document.

Although the MATM is a relatively simple model, finding its posterior distribution over these hidden variables is still intractable. Many efficient approximate inference algorithms have been used to solve this problem including Gibbs sampling (Griffiths and Steyvers, 2004; Steyvers and Griffiths, 2007; Griffiths et al., 2007) and mean-field variational methods (Blei et al., 2003). Gibbs sampling is a special case of Markov-Chain Monte Carlo (MCMC) sampling and often yields relatively simple algorithms for approximate inference in high dimensional models.

In our MATM, we use a collapsed Gibbs sampler for our parameter estimation. In this Gibbs sampler, we integrated out the hidden variables θ and ϕ as shown by the delta function in equation 2. This Dirichlet delta function with a M dimentional symmetric Dirichlet prior is defined in Equation 1. For the current state j, the conditional probability of drawing the kth author K_j^k and the ith topic Z_j^i pair, given all the hyperparameters and all the obeserved documents and authors except the current assignment (the exception is denoted by the symbol $\neg j$), is defined in Equation 2.

$$\Delta_M(\lambda) = \frac{\Gamma(\lambda^M)}{\Gamma(M\lambda)} \tag{1}$$

$$\begin{aligned} & P(Z_j^i, K_j^k | W_j = w, Z_{\neg j}, K_{\neg j}, W_{\neg j}, A_d, \vec{\beta}, \vec{\eta}) \\ & \propto \frac{\Delta(n_Z + \vec{\beta})}{\Delta(n_{Z,\neg j} + \vec{\beta})} \frac{\Delta(n_K + \vec{\eta})}{\Delta(n_{K,\neg j} + \vec{\eta})} \\ & = \frac{n_{i,\neg j}^w + \beta_w}{\sum_{w=1}^V n_{i,\neg j}^w + V\beta_w} \frac{n_{k,\neg j}^i + \vec{\eta_i}}{\sum_{i=1}^T n_{k,\neg j}^i + T\vec{\eta_i}} \end{aligned} \tag{2}$$

And the parameter sets ϕ and θ can be interpreted as sufficient statistics on the state variables of the Markov Chain due to the Dirichlet conjugate priors we used for the multinomial distributions. The two formulars are shown in Equation 3 and Equation 4 in which n_i^w is defined as the number of times that the word w is generated by topic i and n_k^i is defined as the number of times that topic i is generated by author k. The Gibbs sampler used in our experiments is from the Matlab Topic Modeling Toolbox [2].

$$\phi_{w,i} = \frac{n_i^w + \vec{\beta_w}}{\sum_{w=1}^V n_i^w + V\vec{\beta_w}} \tag{3}$$

$$\theta_{k,i} = \frac{n_k^i + \vec{\eta_i}}{\sum_{i=1}^T n_k^i + T\vec{\eta_i}} \tag{4}$$

[2] http://psiexp.ss.uci.edu/research/programs_data/toolbox.htm

4 Experiments and Analysis

In this section, we describe the empirical evaluation of our model qualitatively and quantitatively by applying our model to a text retrieval system we call *Expert Search*. This search engine is intended to retrieve groups of experts with similar interests and expertise by inputting only general domain key words, such as *syntactic parsing, information retrieval*.

We first describe the data set, the retrieval system and the evaluation metrics. Then we present the empirical results both qualitatively and quantitatively.

4.1 Data

We crawled from ACL anthology website and collected seven years of annual ACL conference papers as our corpus. The reference section is deleted from each paper to reduce some noisy vocabulary, such as idiosyncratic proper names, and some coding errors caused during the file format conversion process. We applied a part of speech tagger[3] to tag the files and retain in our vocabulary only content words, i.e., nouns, verbs, adjectives and adverbs.

The ACL anthology website explicitly lists each paper together with its title and author information. Therefore, the author information of each paper can be obtained accurately without extracting from the original paper. We transformed all pdf files to text files and normalized all author names by eliminating their middle name initials if they are present in the listed names. There is a total of 1,326 papers in the collected corpus with $2,084$ authors. Then multiwords (in our current experiments, the bigram collocations) are discovered via the χ^2 statistics and part of speech pattern filtering. These multiwords are then added into the vocabulary to build our model. Some basic statistics about this corpus is summarized in Table 1.

Two sets of results are evaluated use the retrieval system in our experiments: one set is based on unigram vocabulary and the other with the vocabulary expanded by the multiwords.

4.2 Evaluation on Expert Search

We designed a preliminary retrieval system to evaluate our model. The functionality of this search is

[3]The tagger is from:
http://l2r.cs.uiuc.edu/~cogcomp/software.php

ACL Corpus Statistics	
Year range	2003-2009
Total number of papers	1,326
Total number of authors	2,084
Total unigrams	34,012
Total unigram and multiwords	205,260

Table 1: Description of the ACL seven-year collection in our experiments

to associate words with individual authors, i.e., we rank the joint probability of the query words and the target author $P(W, a)$. This probability is marginalized over all topics in the model to rank all authors in our corpus. In addition, the model assumes that the word and the author is conditionally independent given the topic. Formally, we define the ranking function of our retrieval system in Equation 5:

$$\begin{aligned} P(W,a) &= \sum_{w_i} \alpha_i \sum_{t} P(w_i, a|t)P(t) \\ &= \sum_{w_i} \alpha_i \sum_{t} P(w_i|t)P(a|t)P(t) \end{aligned} \quad (5)$$

W is the input query, which may contain one or more words. If a multiword is detected within the query, it is added into the query. The final score is the sum of all words in this query weighted by their inverse document frequency α_i The inverse document frequency is defined as Equation 6.

$$\alpha_i = \frac{1}{DF(w_i)} \quad (6)$$

In our experiments, we chose ten queries which covers several most popular research areas in computational linguistics and natural language processing. In our unigram model, query words are treated token by token. However, in our multiword model, if the query contains a multiword inside our vocabulary, it is treated as an additional token to expand the query. For each query, top 10 authors are returned from the system. We manually label the relevance of these 10 authors based on the papers they submitted to these seven-year ACL conferences collected in our corpus. Two evaluation metrics are used to measure the precision of the retrieving results. First we evaluate the precision at a given cut-off rank, namely precision at K with K ranging from 1 to 10.

We also calculate the average precision (AP) for each query and the mean average precision (MAP) for all the 10 queries. Average precision not only takes ranking as consideration but also emphasizes ranking relevant documents higher. Different from precision at K, it is sensitive to the ranking and captures some recall information since it assumes the precision of the non-retrieved documents to be zero. It is defined as the average of precisions computed at the point of each of the relevant documents in the ranked list as shown in equation 7.

$$AP = \frac{\sum_{r=1}^{n}(Precision(r) \times rel(r))}{\sum relevant\ documents} \quad (7)$$

Currently in our experiments, we do not have a pool of labeled authors to do a good evaluation of recall of our system. However, as in the web browsing activity, many users only care about the first several hits of the retrieving results and precision at K and MAP measurements are robust measurements for this purpose.

4.3 Results and Analysis

In this section, we first examine the qualitative results from our model and then report the evaluation on the external expert search.

4.3.1 Qualitative Coherence Analysis

As have shown by other works on Ngram topic modeling (Wallach, 2006; Wang et al., 2007; Griffiths et al., 2007), our model also demonstrated that embedding multiword tokens into the simple author topic model can always achieve more coherent and better interpretable topics. We list top 15 words from two topics of the multiword model and unigram model respectively in Table 2. Unigram topics contain more general words which can occur in every topic and are usually less discriminative among topics.

Our experiments also show that embedding the multiword tokens into the model achieves better clustering of the authors and the coherence between authors and topics. We demonstrate this qualitatively by listing two examples respectively from the multiword models and the unigram model in Table 3. For example, for the topic on dependency parsing, unigram model missed *Ryan-McDonald* and the ranking of the authors are also questionable. Further

MultiWord Model	**Unigram Model**
TOPIC 4	Topic 51
coreference-resolution	resolution
antecedent	antecedent
treesubstitution-grammars	pronoun
completely	pronouns
pronoun	is
resolution	information
angry	antecedents
candidate	anaphor
extracted	syntactic
feature	semantic
pronouns	coreference
model	anaphora
perceptual-cooccurrence	definite
certain-time	model
anaphora-resolution	only
TOPIC 49	Topic 95
sense	sense
senses	senses
word-sense	disambiguation
target-word	word
word-senses	context
sense-disambiguation	ontext
nouns	ambiguous
automatically	accuracy
semantic-relatedness	nouns
disambiguation	unsupervised
provided	target
ambiguous-word	predominant
concepts	sample
lexical-sample	automatically
nouns-verbs	meaning

Table 2: Comparison of the topic interpretation from the multiword-enhanced and the unigram models. Qualitatively, topics with multiwords are more interpretable.

quantitative measurement is listed in our quantitative evaluation section. However, qualitatively, multiword model seems less problematic.

Some of the unfamiliar author may not be easy to make a relevance judgment. However, if we trace all the papers the author wrote in our collected corpus, many of the authors are coherently related to the topic. We list all the papers in our corpus for three authors from the machine translation topic derived from the multiword model in Table 4 to demonstrate the coherence between the author and the related topic. However, it is also obvious that our model missed some *real* experts in the corresponding field.

MultiWord Model		Unigram Model	
Topic 63	Topic 145	Topic 23	Topic 78
Word	**Word**	**Word**	**Word**
translation	dependency-parsing	translation	dependency
machine-translation	dependency-tree	translations	head
language-model	dependency-trees	bilingual	dependencies
statistical-machine	dependency	pairs	structure
translations	dependency-structures	language	structures
phrases	dependency-graph	machine	dependent
translation-model	dependency-relation	parallel	order
decoding	dependency-relations	translated	word
score	order	monolingual	left
decoder	does	quality	does
Author	**Author**	**Author**	**Author**
Shouxun-Lin	Joakim-Nivre	Hua-Wu	Christopher-Manning
David-Chiang	Jens-Nilsson	Philipp-Koehn	Hisami-Suzuk
Qun-Liu	David-Temperley	Ming-Zhou	Kenji-Sagae
Philipp-Koehn	Wei-He	Shouxun-Lin	Jens-Nilsson
Chi-Ho-Li	Elijah-Mayfield	David-Chiang	Jinxi-Xu
Christoph-Tillmann	Valentin-Jijkoun	Yajuan-Lu	Joakim-Nivre
Chris-Dyer	Christopher-Manning	Haifeng-Wang	Valentin-Jijkoun
G-Haffari	Jiri-Havelka	Aiti-Aw	Elijah-Mayfield
Taro-Watanabe	Ryan-McDonald	Chris-Callison-Burch	David-Temperley
Aiti-Aw	Andre-Martins	Franz-Och	Julia-Hockenmaier

Table 3: Two examples for topic and author coherece from multiword-enhanced model and unigram model. Top 10 words and authors are listed accordingly for each model.

For example, we did not get *Kevin Knight* for the *machine translation* topic. This may be due to the limitation of our corpus since we only collected papers from one conference in a limited time, or because usually these *experts* write more divergent on various topics.

Another observation in our experiment is that some experts with many papers may not be ranked at the very top by our system. However, they have pretty high probability to associate with several topics. Intuitively this makes sense, since many of these famous experts write papers with their students in various topics. Their scores may therefore not be as high as authors who have fewer papers in the corpus which are concentrated in one topic.

4.3.2 Results from Expert Search

One annotator labeled the relevance of the retrieval results from our expert search system. The annotator was also given all the paper titles of each corresponding retrieved author to help make the binary judgment. We experimented with ten queries and retrieved the top ten authors for each query.

We first used the precision at K for evaluation. we calculate the precision at K for both of our multiword model and the unigram model and the results are listed in Table 5. It is obvious that at every rank position, the multiword model works better than the unigram model. In order to focus more on relevant retrieval results, we then calculate the average precision for each query and mean average precision for both models. The results are in Table 6.

When only comparing the mean average precision (MAP), the multiword model works better. However, when examining the average precision of each query within these two models, the unigram model also works pretty well with some queries. How the query words may interact with our model deserves further investigation.

5 Discussion and Further Development

In this paper, we extended the existing author topic model with multiword term-document input and applied it to the domain of expert retrieval. Although our study is preliminary, our experiments do return

Author	Papers from ACL(03-09)
Shouxun-Lin	Log-linear Models for Word Alignment Maximum Entropy Based Phrase Reordering Model for Statistical Machine Translation Tree-to-String Alignment Template for Statistical Machine Translation Forest-to-String Statistical Translation Rules Partial Matching Strategy for Phrase-based Statistical Machine Translation
David-Chiang	A Hierarchical Phrase-Based Model for Statistical Machine Translation Word Sense Disambiguation Improves Statistical Machine Translation Forest Rescoring: Faster Decoding with Integrated Language Models Fast Consensus Decoding over Translation Forests
Philipp-Koehn	Feature-Rich Statistical Translation of Noun Phrases Clause Restructuring for Statistical Machine Translation Moses: Open Source Toolkit for Statistical Machine Translation Enriching Morphologically Poor Languages for Statistical Machine Translation A Web-Based Interactive Computer Aided Translation Tool Topics in Statistical Machine Translation

Table 4: Papers in our ACL corpus for three authors related to the "machine translation" topic in Table 3.

Precision@K		
K	Multiword Model	Unigram Model
1	0.90	0.80
2	0.80	0.80
3	0.73	0.67
4	0.70	0.65
5	0.70	0.64
6	0.72	0.65
7	0.71	0.64
8	0.71	0.66
9	0.71	0.66
10	0.70	0.64

Table 5: Precision at K evaluation of the multiword-enhanced model and the unigram model.

Average Precision (AP)		
Query	Multi. Mod.	Uni. Mod.
Language Model	0.79	0.58
Unsupervised Learning	1.0	0.78
Supervised Learning	0.84	0.74
Machine Translation	0.95	1.0
Semantic Role Labeling	0.81	0.57
Coreference Resolution	0.59	0.72
Hidden Markov Model	0.93	0.37
Dependency Parsing	0.75	0.94
Parsing	0.81	0.98
Transliteration	0.62	0.85
MAP:	**0.81**	0.75

Table 6: Average Precision (AP) for each query and Mean Average Precision (MAP) of the multiword-enhanced model and the unigram model.

promising results, demonstrating the effectiveness of our model in improving coherence in topic clusters. In addition, the use of the MATM for expert retrieval returned some useful preliminary results, which can be further improved in a number of ways.

One immediate improvement would be an extension of our corpus. In our experiments, we considered only ACL papers from the last 7 years. If we extend our data to cover papers from additional conferences, we will be able to strengthen author-topic associations for authors who submit papers on the same topics to different conferences. This will also allow more prominent authors to come to the forefront in our search application. Such a modification would require us to further increase the model's computational efficiency to handle huge volumes of data encountered in real retrieval systems.

Another further development of this paper is the addition of citation information to the model as a layer of supervision for the retrieval system. For instance, an author who is cited frequently could have a higher weight in our system than one who isn't, and could occur more prominently in query results.

Finally, we can provide a better evaluation of our system through a measure of recall and a simple baseline system founded on keyword search of paper titles. Recall can be computed via comparison to a set of expected prominent authors for each query.

Acknowledgments

The research in this paper was supported by the Multimodal Information Access & Synthesis Center at UIUC, part of CCICADA, a DHS Science and Technology Center of Excellence.

References

S. Banerjee and T. Pedersen. 2003. The design, implementation, and use of the Ngram Statistic Package. In *Proceedings of the Fourth International Conference on Intelligent Text Processing and Computational Linguistics*, pages 370–381.

D. Blei and J. Lafferty. 2009a. Topic models. In A. Srivastava and M. Sahami, editors, *Text Mining: Theory and Applications*. Taylor and Francis.

D. Blei and J. Lafferty. 2009b. Visualizing topics with multi-word expressions. In *http://arxiv.org/abs/0907.1013*.

D. Blei, A. Ng, and M. Jordan. 2003. Latent dirichlet allocation. *Journal of Machine Learning Research*.

T. Griffiths and M. Steyvers. 2004. Finding scientific topic. In *Proceedings of the National Academy of Science*.

T. Griffiths, M. Steyvers, and J. Tenenbaum. 2007. Topics in semantic representation. *Psychological Review*.

T. Hofmann. 1999. Probabilistic latent semantic indexing. In *Proceedings of SIGIR*.

J. Justenson and S. Katz. 1995. Technical terminology: some linguistic properties and an algorithm for indentification in text. *Natural Language Engineering*.

D. Magatti, S. Calegari, D. Ciucci, and F. Stella. 2009. Automatic labeling of topics. In *ISDA*, pages 1227–1232.

Christopher D. Manning and Hinrich Schtze. 1999. *Foundations of Statistical Natural Language Processing*. Cambridge, Massachusetts.

Q. Mei, X. Shen, and C. Zhai. 2007. Automatic labeling of multinomial topic models. In *Proceedings of the 13th ACM SIGKDD international conference on Knowledge discovery and data mining*, pages 490–499.

M. Rosen-Zvi, T. Griffiths, M. Steyvers, and P. Smyth. 2004. the author-topic model for authors and documents. In *Proceedings of UAI*.

M. Steyvers and T. Griffiths. 2007. Probabilistic topic models. In *Handbook of Latent Semantic Analysis*. Lawrence Erlbaum Associates.

M. Steyvers, P. Smyth, and T. Griffiths. 2004. Probabilistic author-topic models for information discovery. In *Proceedings of KDD*.

H. Wallach. 2006. Topic modeling; beyond bag of words. In *International Conference on Machine Learning*.

X. Wang and A. McCallum. 2005. A note on topical n-grams. Technical report, University of Massachusetts.

X. Wang, A. McCallum, and X. Wei. 2007. Topical n-grams: Phrase and topic discoery with an application to information retrieval. In *Proceedings of ICDM*.

Query-based Text Normalization Selection Models for Enhanced Retrieval Accuracy

Si-Chi Chin Rhonda DeCook W. Nick Street David Eichmann
The University of Iowa
Iowa City, USA.
{si-chi-chin, rhonda-decook, nick-street, david-eichmann}@uiowa.edu

Abstract

Text normalization transforms words into a base form so that terms from common equivalent classes match. Traditionally, information retrieval systems employ stemming techniques to remove derivational affixes. Depluralization, the transformation of plurals into singular forms, is also used as a low-level text normalization technique to preserve more precise lexical semantics of text.

Experiment results suggest that the choice of text normalization technique should be made individually on each topic to enhance information retrieval accuracy. This paper proposes a hybrid approach, constructing a query-based selection model to select the appropriate text normalization technique (stemming, depluralization, or not doing any text normalization). The selection model utilized ambiguity properties extracted from queries to train a composite of Support Vector Regression (SVR) models to predict a text normalization technique that yields the highest Mean Average Precision (MAP). Based on our study, such a selection model holds promise in improving retrieval accuracy.

1 Introduction

Stemming removes derivational affixes of terms therefore allowing terms from common equivalence classes to be clustered. However, stemming also introduces noise by mapping words of different concepts or meanings into one base form, thus impeding word-sense disambiguation. Depluralization, the conversion of plural word forms to singular form, preserves more precise semantics of text than stemming (Krovetz, 2000).

Empirical research has demonstrated the ambivalent effect of stemming on text retrieval performance. Hull (1996) conducted a comprehensive case study on the effects of four stemmer techniques and the removal of plural "s" [1] on retrieval performance. Hull suggested that the adoption of stemming is beneficial but plural removal is as well competitive when the size of documents is small. Prior research (Manning and Schtze, 1999; McNamee et al., 2008) indicated that traditional stemming, though still benefiting some queries, would not necessarily enhance the average retrieval performance. In addition, stemming was considered one of the technique failures undermining retrieval performance in the TREC 2004 Robust Track (Voorhees, 2006). Prior research also noted the semantic differences between plurals and singulars. Riloff (1995) indicated that plural and singular nouns are distinct because plural nouns usually pertain to the "general types of incidents," while singular nouns often pertain to "a specific incident."

Nevertheless, prior research has not closely examined the effect of the change of the semantics caused by different level of text normalization techniques. In our work, we conducted extensive experiments on the TREC 2004 Robust track collection to evaluate the effect of stemming and depluralization on information retrieval. In addition, we quantify the ambiguity of a query, extracting five ambiguity properties from queries. The extracted ambiguity properties are used to construct query-based selection model, a composite of multiple Support Vector

[1] In our work, we not only removed the plural "s" or "es" but also changed irregular plural forms such as "children" to its singular form "child".

Proceedings of the NAACL HLT 2010 Workshop on Semantic Search, pages 19–26,
Los Angeles, California, June 2010.

Regression models, to determine the most appropriate text normalization technique for a given query. To our knowledge, our work is the first study to construct a query-based selection model, using ambiguity properties extracted from provided queries to select an optimal text normalization technique for each query.

The remainder of this paper is organized as follows. In section 2 we describe our experimental setups and dataset. Section 3 describes and analyzes experiment results of different text normalization techniques on the dataset. We discuss five ambiguity properties and validate each property in section 4. In section 5 we describe the framework and the prediction results of the proposed query-based selection model. Finally, we summarize our findings and discuss future work in section 6.

2 Experiment Setup

The experiment utilizes the queries and relevance judgment results from the TREC 2004 Robust Track to evaluate the effect of three text normalization techniques – raw text, depluralized text, and stemmed text. The TREC 2004 Robust Track used a document set of approximately 528,000 documents comprising 1,904 MB of text. In total, 249 query topics were used in TREC Robust 2004.

Figure 1 illustrates the setup of the experiment. The collection is parsed with a SAX parser and stored in a Postgres database. Lucene is then used to generate three indices: indices of raw text, depluralized text, and stemmed text. The Postgres database stores each document of the collection, the query topics of the TREC 2004 Robust Track, and results of experiments. The ambiguity properties for each query is also computed in the Postgres system. We query Lucene indices to obtain the top 1,000 relevant results and compute Mean Average Precision (MAP) with the trec_eval program to evaluate performance. We use R to analyze performance scores, generate descriptive charts, conduct non-parametric statistical tests, and perform a paired t-test. We use Weka (Hall et al., 2009) to construct query-based selection model that incorporates multiple Support Vector Regression (SVR) models.

2.1 Query Models

The TREC 2004 Robust Track provides 249 query topics; each includes a title, a short description, and a narrative (usually one-paragraph). We selected three basic query models as a modest baseline to demonstrate the effect of different text normalization techniques. Our future work will exploit other ranking models such as BM25 and LMIR. The three query models used in the experiment are: (1) boolean search with the title words of topics concatenated with logical AND (e.g. hydrogen AND fuel AND automobiles); (2) boolean search with the title words of topics concatenated with logical OR (e.g. hydrogen OR fuel OR automobiles); (3) cosine similarity with the title words of topics. Lucene MoreLikeThis (MLT) class supports both boolean and cosine similarity query methods for the experiment. Figure 2 shows how query topics are processed before interrogating the indices. Original queries are first depluralized or stemmed, further processed according to each query model, and finally run against the depluralized and stemmed indices. The experiment runs unprocessed raw queries against the index of raw text, depluralized queries against the index of depluralized text, and stemmed queries against the index of stemmed text.

3 Experiment Results

Table 3 and Figure 3 summarize the results for the full set of topics. Each row in Table 3 represents a query model combined with a given text normalization technique as described in section 2.1.

For each query model and text normalization technique, we present the MAP value computed across all relevant topics. We also provide the p-value for comparing MAP between each normalization technique and the baseline (i.e. non-normalized (raw) queries). The p-value is generated from the pairwise Wilcoxon signed rank sum test. Figure 3 describes the distribution of MAP across the three text normalization techniques and three query models. The distributions are skewed and many outliers are observed. In general, boolean OR and MLT query models perform similarly and stemming has the highest median MAP value across all three query models. The results from Table 3 for the combined topic set show that depluralization and stemming perform significantly better than the raw baseline. However, the performance difference between depluralization and stemming is not significant except for the AND boolean query model. In general, the differences of MAP among three text normalization

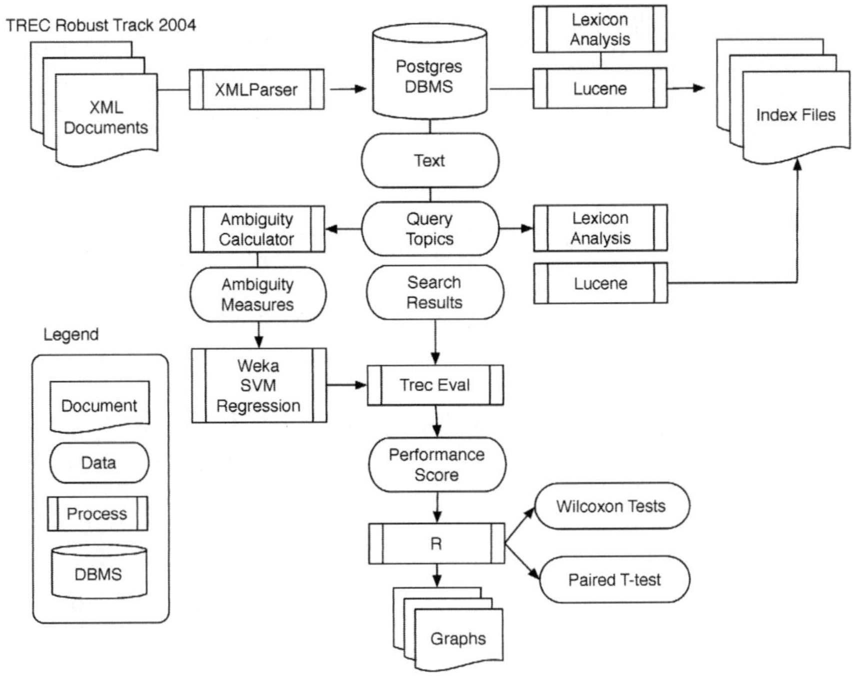

Figure 1: Flow chart of experiment setup

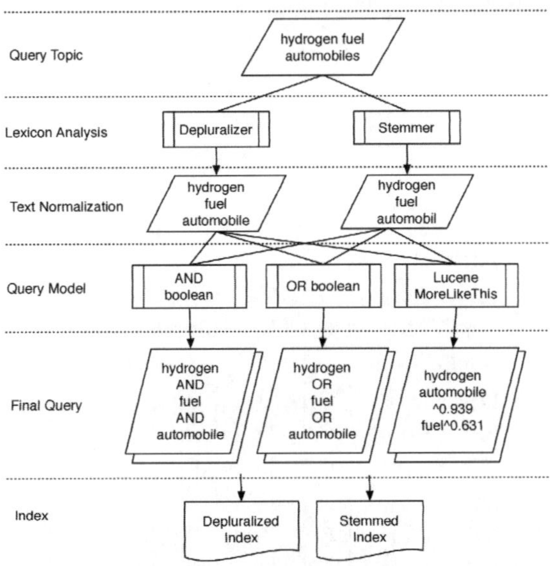

Figure 2: Using the query "hydrogen fuel automobiles" as an example, the depluralized query becomes "hydrogen fuel automobile" and the stemmed query becomes "hydrogen fuel automobil." Final boolean queries for depluralized topic become "hydrogen AND fuel AND automobile" and "hydrogen OR fuel OR automobil." MoreLikeThis (MLT) is the Lucene class used for cosine similarity retrieval. A term vector score appends each word in the topic.

techniques are within 2%.

To visualize the relative performances among three text normalization techniques, we standardized the three MAP values for a single topic (one from each text normalization technique) to have mean 0 and standard deviation of 1. The result provides a 3-value pattern emphasizing the ordering of the MAPs across the text normalization techniques, rather than the raw MAP values themselves. We then used the K-medoids algorithm (Kaufman and Rousseeuw, 1990) to cluster the transformed data, applying Euclidean distance as the distance measure. Figure 4 is an example of 9 constructed clusters based on the MAP scores of the MLT query model. In a cluster, a line represents the standardized MAP value of a topic on each text normalization technique. Given the small differences in aggregate MAP performance, it is interesting to note that the clusters demonstrate variable patterns, indicating that some topics performed better as a depluralized query than a stemmed query.

The cluster analysis suggests that the choice of text normalization technique should be made individually on each topic. As we choose an appropriate text normalization technique for a given topic, we would further enhance retrieval performance. In

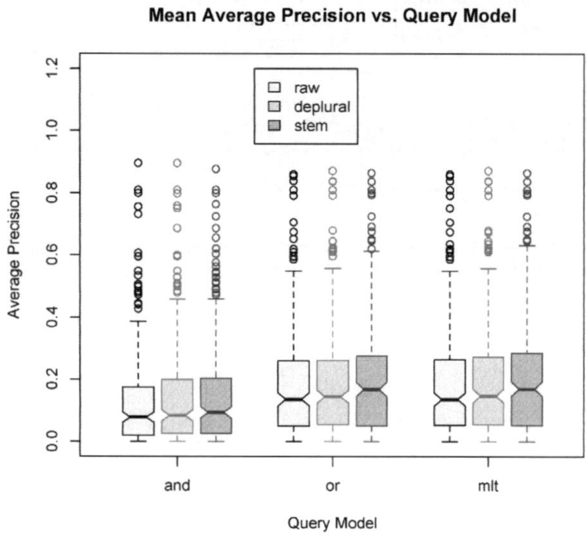

Figure 3: Profile plot of MAP

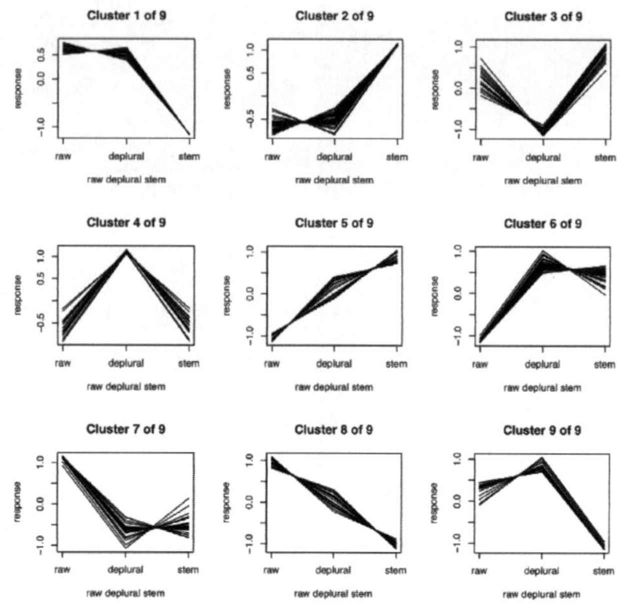

Figure 4: Example of relative performance similarities among text normalization techniques. The cluster analysis uses the MAP scores of the MLT query model

the next section, we address the issue of inconsistent performance by constructing regression models to predict the mean average precision of each query from the ambiguity measures, and choose an appropriate normalization method based on these predictions.

4 Ambiguity Properties

Research has affirmed the negative impact of query ambiguity on an information retrieval system. As stemming clusters terms of different concepts, it should increase query ambiguity. To quantify the query ambiguity potentially caused by stemming, we compute five ambiguity properties for each query: 1) the product of the number of senses, referred as the sense product; 2) the product of the number of words mapped to one base form (e.g. a stem), referred as the word product; 3) the ratio of the sense product of depluralized query to which of stemmed query, referred as the deplural-stem ratio; 4) the sum of the inverse document frequency for each word in a query, referred as the idf-sum; 5) the length of a query.

4.1 Sense Product

Sense product measures the extent of query ambiguity after stemming. We first find all words mapped to a given stem and, for each word, we then count the number of senses found in WordNet. To compute

	Combined Topic Set	
Run	MAP	p-value
AND_Raw	0.1213	N/A
AND_Dep	0.1324	5.598e-06*
AND_Stem	0.1550 †	1.599e-07*
OR_Raw	0.1851	N/A
OR_Dep	0.1922	0.03035*
OR_Stem	0.2069	0.01123*
MLT_Raw	0.1893	N/A
MLT_Dep	0.1959	0.04837*
MLT_Stem	0.2093	0.009955*

Table 1: Paired Wilcoxon signed-ranked test on Mean Average Precision (MAP), utilizing raw query as the baseline. Significant differences between query models are labeled with *. Results labeled with † indicate significant differences between depluralized queries and a stemmed queries.

the number of senses for a given stem, we accumulate the number of senses of each word mapped to the stem. The sense product is then the multiplying of the number of senses for each stemmed query term, computed as:

$$sense\_product = \prod_{i=1}^{n} \sum_{j=1}^{m} S_j \qquad (1)$$

S_j denotes the number of senses for each word mapped to a stem i. We have m words mapped to a stem i and have n stems in a query. As the sense product increases, the query ambiguity increases. Figure 5 illustrates the computation of the sense product for the query "organic soil enhancement." The term "organic" has the stem organ, which is a stem for 9 different words. The accumulated number of senses for "organ" is 39. With the same approach, we obtain 7 senses for 1 "soil" and 7 senses for "enhanc." Therefore, multiplication 39, 7, and 7 gives us the sense product value 1911.

4.2 Word Product

Word product is an alternative measure of query ambiguity after stemming. To compute the word product, we multiply the number of words mapped to each stem of a given query, which is formulated as:

$$word\_product = \prod_{i=1}^{n} W_i \qquad (2)$$

W_i denotes the number of words mapped to a stem i, and n is the number of stems in a query. We assume that the query ambiguity increases as the word product increases. Consider the query "organic soil enhancement" in Figure 5. We find 9 words mapped to the stem "organ"; 3 words mapped to the stem "soil"; 5 words mapped to the stem "enhancement". Therefore the word product for the query is 105, the product of 9, 3, and 5.

4.3 Deplural-Stem Ratio

Deplural-stem ratio is a variation of sense product. It takes the ratio of the sense product of a depluralized query to the stemmed query. As the deplural-stem ratio increases, the query ambiguity after stemming increases. In the example illustrated in Figure 5, the deplural-stem ratio is the sense product of the depluralized query "organic soil enhancement" divided by the sense product of the stemmed query "organ soil enhanc". The deplural-stem ratio is computed as:

$$deplural\text{-}stem\_ratio = \frac{\prod_{i=1}^{n} \sum_{j=1}^{m} Sm_j}{\prod_{i=1}^{n} \sum_{j=1}^{m} D_j} \qquad (3)$$

4.4 Idf-sum

The idf-sum is the sum of the inverse document frequency (IDF) of each word in the query. The IDF of a given word measures the importance of the word in the document collection. Queries with high values of IDF are more likely to return relevant documents from the collection. For example, the term "ZX-Turbo," describing a series of racing cars, has a high IDF and occurs only once in the entire TREC 2004 Robust Track collection. Therefore, searching the collection with the term "ZX-Turb" will return the only relevant document in the collection and achieve high precision and recall. The idf-sum is computed as:

$$idf\_sum = \sum_{i=1}^{n} IDF_i \qquad (4)$$

IDF_i denotes the idf of each query term i and n is the number of words in a query. We assume that the query ambiguity decreases as the idf-sum increases. For the query "organic soil enhancement", the IDF for each term is 5.97082 (organic), 5.18994 (soil), and 4.86996 (enhancement). The idf-sum of the query is 16.0307.

4.5 Query Length

The length of the query is the number of words in a query.

4.6 Feature Validation

We performed simple linear regression on each feature as the first step to exclude ineffectual features. Table 2 demonstrates example results of simple linear regression from the MLT query model, using the MAP of stemmed queries as the dependent variable. We take the logarithm of the sense product and word product and the square root of the deplural-stem ratio (ds_ratio) to mitigate skewness of the data. We included all five ambiguity properties to construct a query-based selection model as they demonstrate statistical significance in prediction.

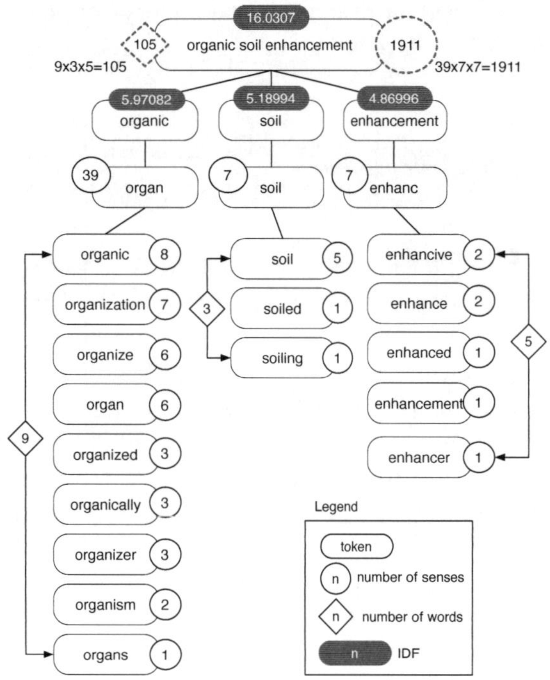

Figure 5: Example of ambiguity indicators on the query "organic soil enhancement"

Figure 6 demonstrates the distribution of ambiguity properties against the actual best text normalization technique. It is noted that stemming is the actual best method when a query has lower sense product, or lower word product, or a higher idf-sum. It implies that stemming is less likely to be the actual best method as a query is ambiguous. The results demonstrate the potential of utilizing ambiguity measures to select the actual best text normalization technique.

5 Query-based Selection Model

The cluster analysis in Section 3 suggests that the choice of text normalization technique should be made individually on each topic. The retrieval performance would be enhanced as we choose an appropriate text normalization technique for a given topic. Given the five ambiguity properties described in Section 4, we constructed Support Vector Regression (SVR) (Smola and Schlkopf, 2004) models to choose between stemming, depluralization, and not doing any text normalization for different queries. Regression models aim to discover the relationship between two random variables x and y. In our work, independent variable x is a vector of the five properties described in section 4: x = *(sense_product, word_product, deplural-stem_ratio, Idf-sum, length)*, and dependent variable y is the MAP score of a given topic. SVR has been successfully applied for many time series and function estimation problems. We utilized training data to construct multiple SVR models for each of nine combinations of query models (AND, OR, and MLT) and text normalization techniques (raw, depluralized, and stemmed queries). For example, the regression model for an MLT query model using stemmed queries is:

$$\begin{aligned} Map\_MLT\_stem = {} & 0.0853 \\ & - 0.0849 * length \\ & + 0.6286 * sense\_prod \\ & + 0.0171 * word\_prod \\ & - 0.0774 * gap\_ds \\ & + 0.4189 * idf\_sum \end{aligned}$$

For a given query model, MLT, for example, we utilized training data to construct three SVR models each to predict the MAP scores of raw queries, depluralized queries, and stemmed queries in the test set. We then compared the predicted MAP score of a query and selected the text normalization technique with the highest predicted score. Figure 5 illustrates our experiment framework on the query-based selection model. We used five-fold cross-validation to evaluate the performance of the selection model. For each iteration (fold) we used the 4 out of the 5 partitions as training data, constructing SVR models and using the remaining fifth partition for testing. We accumulated all testing results and computed one overall MAP score for evaluation. Table 3 shows the results of the five-fold cross-validation performed on 249 query topics provided by the TREC 2004 Robust Track. We utilized a paired t-test to determine the performance difference between the query-based selection model (hybrid model) and other three text normalization techniques. The results in Table 3 shows that the query-based selection model attained the highest MAP score and achieved significant improvement.

6 Conclusion and Future work

This paper evaluates the performance of stemming and depluralization on the TREC 2004 Robust track collection. We assume that the depluralization, as

Feature	Coefficient	R-square	P-value
length	-0.06811	0.07864	5.768e-05*
log(sense_prod)	-0.034692	0.1482	1.819e-08*
log(word_prod)	-0.04557	0.09426	9.78e-06*
sqrt(ds_ratio)	-0.021657	0.03738	0.006088*
idf_sum	0.008498	0.04165	0.003747*

Table 2: Results of simple linear regression on the MAP of stemmed queries in MLT query model.

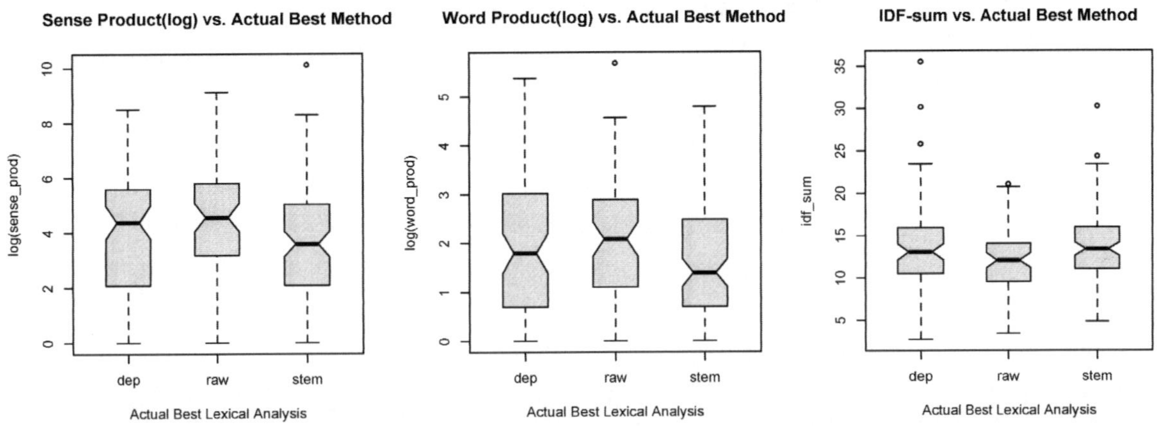

Figure 6: Boxplots of the distribution of three ambiguity properties in each actual best text normalization technique

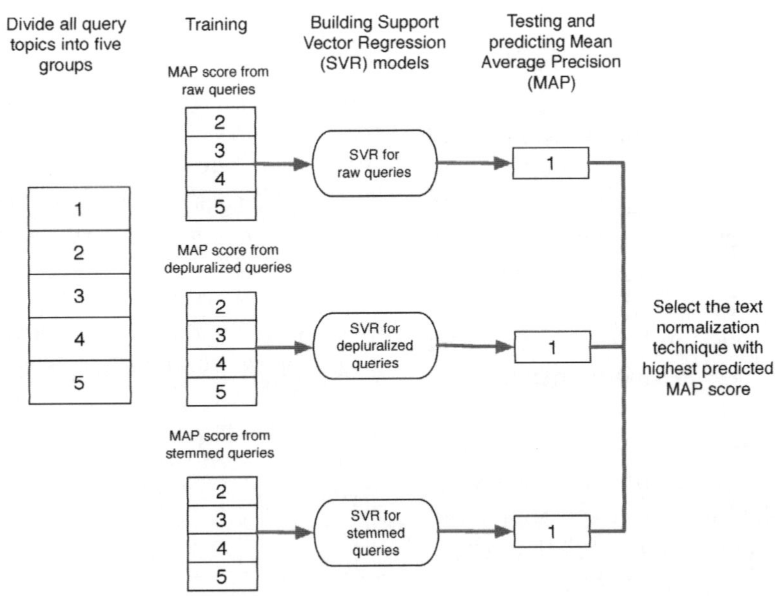

Figure 7: Five-fold cross validation on query-based selection model (hybrid model)

		Raw	Dep	Stem	Hybrid
AND	MAP	**0.1213**	**0.1324**	**0.1550**	**0.2094**
	p-value	<2.2e-16*	<2.2e-16*	<2.2e-16*	
OR	MAP	**0.1851**	**0.1922**	0.2069	**0.2131**
	p-value	1.286e-05*	0.0003815*	0.09	
MLT	MAP	**0.1893**	**0.1959**	0.2093	**0.2132**
	p-value	3.979e-05*	0.000939*	0.09677	

Table 3: Paired T-test was performed to examine the differences of each text normalization techniques (raw, depluralizer, and stemmer) and query-based selection model (hybrid model). Significant differences between models are labeled with *.

a low-level text-normalization technique, introduces less ambiguity than stemming and preserves more precise semantics of text. The experimental results demonstrate variable patterns, indicating that some topics performed better as a depluralized query than as a stemmed query. From Figure 4 in Section 3, we conclude that the choice of text normalization technique should be made individually on each topic. An effective query-based selection model would enhance information retrieval performance. The query-based selection model utilizes Support Vector Regression (SVR) models to predict the mean average precision (MAP) of each query from the ambiguity measures, and to choose an appropriate normalization technique based on these predictions. The selection is lightweight, requiring only analysis of the topic title itself against information readily available regarding the corpus (e.g, term idf values). We extracted 5 measures to quantify the ambiguity of a query: 1) sense product; 2) word product; 3) deplural-stem ratio; 4) idf-sum; 5) length of a query. The constructed query-based selection model demonstrate positive results on enhanced performance. The experiments reported here show that, even when the improvement is modest (1%), the selection model competes well with traditional approaches. To improve the model, future work may first explore and introduce more powerful features to the models, considering properties such as part of speech of text. Second, future work may explore the effect of noise and outliers in the data to improve the accuracy of the model. Finally, additional data mining techniques may be adopted in future work to further improve the prediction.

References

M. Hall, E. Frank, G. Holmes, B. Pfahringer, P. Reutemann, and I.H. Witten. 2009. The WEKA Data Mining Software: An Update. *SIGKDD Explorations*, 1:10–18.

David A. Hull. 1996. Stemming algorithms: A case study for detailed evaluation. *Journal of the American Society for Information Science*, 47(1):70–84.

L. Kaufman and P.J. Rousseeuw. 1990. *Finding groups in data. An introduction to cluster analysis*. Wiley, New York.

Robert Krovetz. 2000. Viewing morphology as an inference process. *Artificial Intelligence*, 118(1-2):277–294, April.

Christopher D Manning and Hinrich Schtze. 1999. *Foundations of Statistical Natural Language Processing*. MIT Press, Cambridge, Mass.

Paul McNamee, Charles Nicholas, and James Mayfield. 2008. Don't have a stemmer?: be un+concern+ed. In *Proceedings of the 31st International ACM SIGIR Conference on Research and Development in Information retrieval*, pages 813–814, Singapore, Singapore. ACM.

Ellen Riloff. 1995. Little words can make a big difference for text classification. In *Proceedings of the 18th International ACM SIGIR Conference on Research and Development in Information Retrieval*, pages 130–136, Seattle, Washington, United States. ACM.

Alex J. Smola and Bernhard Schlkopf. 2004. A tutorial on support vector regression. *Statistics and Computing*, 14(3):199–222.

E. M. Voorhees. 2006. The TREC 2005 robust track. In *ACM SIGIR Forum*, volume 40, pages 41–48. ACM New York, NY, USA.

A Graph-Based Semi-Supervised Learning for Question Semantic Labeling

Asli Celikyilmaz
Computer Science Division
University of California, Berkeley
asli@berkeley.edu

Dilek Hakkani-Tur
International Computer Science Institute
Berkeley, CA
dilek@icsi.berkeley.edu

Abstract

We investigate a graph-based semi-supervised learning approach for labeling semantic components of questions such as *topic, focus, event, etc.*, for question understanding task. We focus on graph construction to handle learning with dense/sparse graphs and present *Relaxed Linear Neighborhoods* method, in which each node is linearly constructed from varying sizes of its neighbors based on the density/sparsity of its surrounding. With the new graph representation, we show performance improvements on syntactic and real datasets, primarily due to the use of unlabeled data and relaxed graph construction.

1 Introduction

One of the important steps in Question Answering (QA) is *question understanding* to identify semantic components of questions. In this paper, we investigate question understanding based on a machine learning approach to discover semantic components (Table 1).

$\underbrace{What}_{other}\ \underbrace{film}_{focus}\ \underbrace{introduced}_{event}\ \underbrace{Jar\ Jar\ Binks}_{topic}?$
Semantic Components & Named-Entitiy Types
topic: *'Jar' (Begin-Topic); 'Jar' (In-Topic) ; 'Binks' (In-Topic)(HUMAN:Individual)*
focus: *'film' (Begin-Focus) (DESCRIPTION:Definition)*
action / event: *'introduced' (Begin-Event)*
expected answer-type: *ENTITY:creative*

Table 1: Question Analysis - Semantic Components of a sample question from TREC QA task.

An important issue in information extraction from text is that one often deals with insufficient labeled data and large number of unlabeled data, which have led to improvements in semi-supervised learning (SSL) methods, e.g., (Belkin and Niyogi., 2002b), (Zhou et al., 2004). Recently, graph based SSL methods have gained interest (Alexandrescu and Kirchhoff, 2007), (Goldberg and Zhu, 2009). These methods create graphs whose vertices correspond to labeled and unlabeled data, while the edge weights encode the similarity between each pair of data points. Classification is performed using these graphs by scoring unlabeled points in such a way that instances connected by large weights are given similar labels. Such methods can perform well when no parametric information about distribution of data is available and when data is characterized by an underlying manifold structure.

In this paper, we present a semantic component labeling module for our QA system using a new graph-based SSL to benefit from unlabeled questions. One of the issues affecting the performance of graph-based methods (Maier and Luxburg, 2008) is that there is no reliable approach for model selection when there are too few labeled points (Zhou et al., 2004). Such issues have only recently came into focus (Wang and Zhang, 2006). This is somewhat surprising because *graph construction* is a fundamental step. Rather than proposing yet another learning algorithm, we focus on graph construction for our labeling task, which suffers from insufficient graph sparsification methods. Such problems are caused by fixed neighborhood assignments in k-nearest neighbor approaches, treating sparse and denser regions of data equally or using improper threshold assumptions in ϵ-neighborhood

Proceedings of the NAACL HLT 2010 Workshop on Semantic Search, pages 27–35,
Los Angeles, California, June 2010.

graphs, yielding disconnected components or subgraphs or isolated singleton vertices. We propose a *Relaxed Linear Neighborhood* (RLN) method to overcome fixed k or ϵ assumptions. RLN approximates the entire graph by a series of overlapped linear neighborhood patches, where neighborhood $\mathcal{N}(x_i)$ of any node x_i is captured dynamically based on the density/sparsity of its surrounding. Moreover, RLN exploits *degree of neighborhood* during reconstruction method rather than fixed assignments, which does not get affected by outliers, producing a more robust graph, demonstrated in Experiment #1.

We present our question semantic component model in section 3 with the following contributions:
(1) a new *graph construction* method for SSL, which relaxes neighborhood assumptions yielding robust graphs as defined in section 5,
(2) a new *inference approach* to enable learning from unlabeled data as defined in section 6.
The experiments in section 7 yield performance improvement in comparison to other labeling methods on different datasets. Finally we draw conclusions.

2 Related Work on Question Analysis

An important step in question analysis is extracting semantic components like *answer type, focus, event*, etc. The 'answer-type' is a quantity that a question is seeking. A question *'topic'* usually represents major context/constraint of a question ("Jar Jar Binks" in Table 1). A question *'focus'* (e.g., film) denotes a certain aspect (or descriptive feature) of a question *'topic'*. To extract topic-focus from questions, (Hajicova et al., 1993) used rule-based approaches via dependency parser structures. (Burger, 2006) implemented parsers and a mixture of rule-based and learning methods to extract different salient features such as question type, event, entities, etc. (Chai and Jin, 2004) explored semantic units based on their discourse relations via rule-based systems.

In (Duan et al., 2008) a language model is presented to extract semantic components from questions. Similarly, (Fan et al., 2008)'s semantic chunk annotation uses conditional random fields (CRF) (Lafferty et al., 2001) to annotate semantic chunks of questions in Chinese. Our work aparts from these studies in that we use a graph-based SSL method to extract semantic components from unlabeled questions. Graph-based methods are suitable for labeling tasks because when two lexical units in different questions are close in the intrinsic geometry of question forms, their semantic components (labels) will be similar to each other. Labels vary smoothly along the geodesics, i.e., manifold assumption, which plays an essential role in SSL (Belkin et al., 2006).

This paper presents a new graph construction to improve performance of an important module of QA when labeled data is sparse. We compare our results with other graph construction methods. Next, we present the dataset construction for our semantic component labeling model before we introduce the new graph construction and inference for SSL.

3 Semantic Component Labeling

Each word (token) in a question is associated with a label among a pre-determined list of semantic tags. A question i is defined as a sequence of input units (words/tokens) $x_i = (x_{1i}, ..., x_{Ti}) \in \mathcal{X}^T$ which are tagged with a sequence of class labels, $y_i = (y_{1i}, ..., y_{Ti}) \in \mathcal{Y}^T$, semantic components. The task is to learn classifier $\mathcal{F}$ that, given a new sequence x^{new}, predicts a sequence of class labels $y^{new} = \mathcal{F}(x^{new})$. Among different semantic component types presented in previous studies, we give each token a MUC style semantic label from a list of 11 labels.
(1) O: $other$;
(2) BT:*begin-topic*;
(3) IT:*in-topic*
(4) BF:*begin-focus*;
(5) IF:*in-focus*
(6) BE:*begin-event*;
(7) IE:*in-event*
(8) BCL:*begin-clause*
(9) ICL:*in-clause*
(10) BC:*begin-complement*
(11) IC:*in-complement*
More labels can be appended if necessary. The first token of a component gets *'begin'* prefix and consecutive words are given *'in'* prefix, e.g., *Jar (begin-topic), Jar (in-topic), Binks (in-topic)* in Table 1.

In graph-based SSL methods, a graph is constructed $\mathcal{G} = \langle \mathcal{V}, \mathcal{E} \rangle$, where $\mathcal{V} = \mathcal{X}$ is a vertex set, $\mathcal{E}$ is an edge set, associated with each edge e_{ij} represents a relation between x_i and x_j. The task is to assign a label (out of 11 possible labels) to each token of a question i, x_{ti}, $t = 1, ..., T$, T is the max number of tokens in a given query. We introduce a set of nodes for each token (x_{ti}), each representing a binary relation between that token and one of possible tags (y_{ti}). A binary relation represents an agreement between a given token and assigned label, so our SSL classifier predicts the probability of true relation between token and assigned label. Thus, for each token, we introduce 11 different nodes using $y_k \in \{O,BT,IT,BF,IF,BC,IC,BE,IE,BCL,ICL\}$. There will be 11 label probability assignments obtained from each of the 11 corresponding nodes. For labeled questions, intuitively, only one node per token is introduced to the graph for known(true) token/label relations. We find the best question label sequence via Viterbi algorithm (Forney, 1973).

3.1 Feature Extraction For Labeling Task

The following pre-processing modules are built for feature extraction prior to graph construction.

3.1.1 Pre-Processing For Feature Extraction

Phrase Analysis(PA): Using basic syntactic analysis (shallow parsing), the PA module re-builds phrases from linguistic structures such as noun-phrases (NN), basic prepositional phrases (PP) or verb groups (VG). Using Stanford dependency parser (Klein and Manning, 2003), (Marneffe et al., 2006), which produces 48 different grammatical relations, PA module re-constructs the phrases. For example for the question in Table 1, dependency parser generates two relations:
– *nn(Binks-3, Jar-1)* and *nn(Binks-3, Jar-2)*,
PA reveals *"Jar Jar Binks"* as a noun phrase reconstructing the ***nn****:noun compound modifier*. We also extract part of speech tags of questions via dependency parser to be used for feature extraction.

Question Dependency Relations (QDR): Using shallow semantics, we decode underlying Stanford dependency trees (Marneffe et al., 2006) that embody linguistic relationships such as head-subject (H-S), head-modifier (complement) (H-M), head-object (H-O), etc. For example: *"How did Troops enter the area last Friday?"* is chunked as:
– Head (H): *enter* – Object (O): *area*
– Subject (S): *Troops* – Modifier (M): *last Friday*

Later, the feature functions (FF) are extracted based on generalized rules such as S and O's are usually considered topic/focus, H is usually an event, etc.

3.1.2 Features for Token-Label Pairs

Each node v_i in a graph $\mathcal{G}$ represents a relation of any token(word) i, x_{ti} to its label y_{ti}, denoted as a feature vector $x_{ti} \in \Re^d$. A list of feature functions are formed to construct multi-dimensional training examples. We extract mainly first and second order features to identify token-label relations, as follows:

Lexicon Features (LF): These features are over words and their labels along with information about words such as POS tags, etc. A sample first order lexicon feature, $z(y_t, x_{1:T}, t)$:

$$z = \begin{cases} 1 & \text{if } y_t = \text{(BE/IE) and POS}_{x_t}\text{=VB} \\ 0 & \text{otherwise} \end{cases} \quad (1)$$

is set to 1, if its assigned label y_t is of event type (BE/IE) and word's POS tag is VB(verb) (such token-label assignment would be correct). A similar feature is set to 1 if a word has 'VB' as its POS tag and it is a copula word, so it's correct label can only be "O:other". Nodes satisfying only this constraint and have a relation to "O" label get the value of '1'. Similar binary features are: if the word is a WH type (*query word*), if its POS tag is an article, if its POS tag is NN(P)(noun), IN, etc.

Compound Features (CF): These features exploit semantic compound information obtained from our PA and QDR modules, in which noun-phrases are labeled as focus/topics, or verb-phrases as event. For instance, if a token is part of a semantic compound, e.g., *subject*, identified via our QDR module, then for any of the 11 nodes generated for this token, if token-label is other than 'O(Other)', then such feature would be 1, and 0 otherwise. Similarly, if a word is part of a noun-phrase, then a node having a relation to any of the labels other than 'O/BE/IE' would be given the value 1, and 0 otherwise We eliminate inclusion of some nodes with certain labels such as words with "NN" tags are not usually considered *events*.

Probability Feature Functions (PFF): We calculate word unigram and bigram frequencies from training samples to extract label conditional probabilities given a word, e.g., *P*(BT—"IBM"), *P*(O-BE—"Who founded"). When no match is found in unigram and bigram label conditional probability tables for testing cases, we use unigram and bigram label probabilities given the POS tag of that word, e.g., *P*(BT—NNP), *P*(O-BE—"WP-VBD"). We extract 11 different features for each word corresponding to each possible label to form the probability features from unigram frequencies, max. of 11X11 features for bigram frequencies, where some bigrams are never seen in training dataset.

Second-Order Features (SOF): Such features denote relation between a token, tag and tag$_{-1}$, e.g.,:

$$z = \begin{cases} 1 & \text{if } y_{t-1} = \text{BT}, y_t = \text{IT and POS}_{x_t} = \text{NN} \\ 0 & \text{otherwise} \end{cases} \tag{2}$$

which indicates if previous label is a start of a topic tag (BT) and current POS tag is NN, then a node with a relation to label "In-Topic (IT)" would yield value '1'. For any given token, one should introduce 11^2 different nodes to represent a single property. In experiments we found that only a limited number of second order nodes are feasible.

4 Graph Construction for SSL

Let $\mathcal{X}_L = \{x_1, ..., x_l\}$ be labeled question tokens with associated labels $Y_L = \{y_1, ..., y_l\}^T$ and $\mathcal{X}_U = \{x_1, ..., x_u\}$ be unlabeled tokens, $\mathcal{X} = \mathcal{X}_L \cup \mathcal{X}_U$.

A weighted symmetric adjacency matrix $\mathcal{W}$ is formed in two steps with edges E in $\mathcal{G}$ where $\mathcal{W}_{ij} \in \Re^{nxn}$, and non-zero elements represent the edge weight between v_i and v_j. Firstly, similarity between each pair of nodes is obtained by a measure to create a full affinity matrix, $\mathcal{A} \in \Re^{nxn}$, using a kernel function, $\mathcal{A}_{ij} = k(x_i, x_j)$ as weight measure (Zhou et al., 2004) $w_{ij} \in \Re^{n \times n}$:

$$w_{ij} = exp\left(- \|x_i - x_j\| / 2\sigma^2\right) \tag{3}$$

Secondly, based on chosen graph sparsification method, a sparse affinity matrix is obtained by removing edges that do not convey with neighborhood assumption. Usually a k-nearest neighbor (kNN) or ϵ neighbor (ϵN) methods are used for sparsification.

Graph formation is crucial in graph based SSL since sparsity ensures that the predicted model remains efficient and robust to noise, e.g., especially in text processing noise is inevitable. ϵN graphs provide weaker performance than the k-nearest neighborhood graphs (Jebara et al., 2009). In addition, the issue with kNN sparsification of graph is that the number of neighbors is fixed at the start, which may cause fault neighborhood assumptions even when neighbors are far apart. Additionally, kernel similarity functions may not rate edge weights because they might be useful locally but not quite efficient when nodes are far apart. Next, we present *Relaxed Linear Neighborhoods* to address these issues.

5 Relaxed Linear Neighborhoods (RLN)

Instead of measuring pairwise relations (3), we use neighborhood information to construct $\mathcal{G}$. When building a sparse affinity matrix, we re-construct each node using a linear combination of its neighbors, similar to *Locally Linear Embedding* (Roweis and Saul, 2000) and *Linear Neighborhoods* (Wang and Zhang, 2006), and minimize:

$$\min \textstyle\sum_i ||x_i - \sum_{j:x_j \in \mathcal{N}(x_i)} w_{ij} x_j||^2 \tag{4}$$

where $\mathcal{N}(x_i)$ is neighborhood of x_i, and w_{ij} is the degree of contribution of x_j to x_i. In (4) each node can be optimally reconstructed using a linear combination of its neighborhood (Roweis and Saul, 2000). However, having fixed k neighbors at start of the algorithm can effect generalization of classifier and can also cause confusion on different manifolds.

We present novel *RLN* method to reconstruct each object (node) by using dynamic neighborhood information, as opposed to fixed k neighbors of (Wang and Zhang, 2006). RLN approximates entire graph by a series of overlapped *linear neighborhood patches*, where neighborhood $\mathcal{N}(x_i)$ of a node x_i is captured dynamically via its neighbor's density.

Boundary Detection: Instead of finding fixed k neighbors of each node x_i (Wang and Zhang, 2006), RLN captures boundary of each node $\mathcal{B}(x_i)$ based on neighborhood information and pins each node within this boundary as its neighbors. We define weight $\mathcal{W}$ matrix using a measure like (3) as a first pass sparsification. We identify neighbors for each node $x_i \in X$ and save information in boundary matrix, $\mathcal{B}$. kNN recovers its k neighbors using a similarity function, e.g., a kernel distance function, and instantiates via:

$$\mathcal{N}_{x_i;k}(x_j) = \left\{ \begin{array}{ll} 1 & d(x_i, x_{j_1}) < d(x_i, x_{j_2}) \\ 0 & otherwise \end{array} \right\} \tag{5}$$

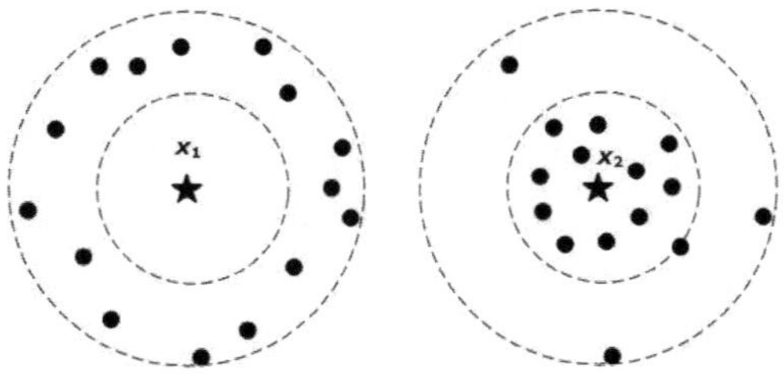

Figure 1: Neighborhood Boundary. Having same number of neighbors (n=15), boundaries of x_1 and x_2 are similar based on kNN (e.g., k=15), but dissimilar based on ϵN.

Similarly, with the ϵN approach the neighbors are instantiated when they are at most ϵ far away:

$$\mathcal{N}_{x_i;\epsilon}(x_j) = \left\{ \begin{array}{ll} 1 & d(x_i, x_j) < \epsilon \\ 0 & otherwise \end{array} \right\} \quad (6)$$

Both methods have limitations when sparsity or density is to concern. For sparse regions, if we restrict definition to k neighbors, then $\mathcal{N}(x_i)$ would contain dissimilar points. Similarly, improper threshold values could result in disconnected components or subgraphs or isolated singleton vertices. ϵ-radius would not define a graph because not every neighborhood radius would have the same density (see Fig. 1). Neighborhoods of two points (x_1, x_2) are different, although they contain same number of nodes.

We can use both *kNN* and ϵNN approaches to define the neighborhood between any x_i and x_j as:

$$\mathcal{N}_{x_i;k,\epsilon}(x_j) = \left\{ \begin{array}{ll} 1 & |\mathcal{N}_\epsilon(x_i)| > k \\ \mathcal{N}_{x_i;k}(x_j) & otherwise \end{array} \right\} \quad (7)$$

$|\mathcal{N}_\epsilon(x_i)|$ denotes cardinality of ϵ-neighbors of x_i, and $\mathcal{N}_{x_i;k}(x_j) \in \{0, 1\}$ according to (5). Thus if there are enough number of nodes in the ϵ vicinity ($> k$), then the boundary is identified. Otherwise we use kNN. Boundary set of any x_i is defined as:

$$\mathcal{B}(x_i) = \left\{ x_{j=1..n} \in X \,\middle|\, \mathcal{I}_{\mathcal{N}_{x_i;k,\epsilon}(x_j)=1} \right\} \quad (8)$$

Relaxed Boundary Detection: Adjusting boundaries based on a neighborhood radius and density might cause some problems. Specifically, if dense regions (clusters) exist and parameters are set large for sparse datasets, e.g., k and ϵ, then neighborhood sets would include more (and even noisy) nodes than necessary. Similarly, for low density regions if parameters are set for dense neighborhoods, weak neighborhood bonds will be formed to re-construct via linear neighborhoods. An algorithm that can handle a wide range of change interval would be advantageous. It should also include information provided by neighboring nodes closest to the corresponding node, which can take neighborhood relation into consideration more sensitively. Thus we extend neighborhood definition in (7) and (8) accounting for sensitivity of points with varying distances to neighbor points based on parameter $k > 0$:

$$\mathcal{N}_{x_i}(x_j) = max\left\{(1 - k\left(d(x_i, x_j)/d_{max}\right)), 0\right\} \quad (9)$$

$$\begin{array}{l} d_{max} = \max_{x_i, x_j \in X} d(x_i, x_j) \\ d(x_i, x_j) = \sqrt{\sum_{p=1}^{m} (x_{ip} - x_{jp})^2} \end{array} \quad (10)$$

In (10) m is the max. feature vector dimension of any x_i, k plays a role in determining neighborhood radius, such that it could be adjusted as follows:

$$1 - k\left(\epsilon/d_{max}\right) = 0 \Rightarrow k = d_{max}/\epsilon \quad (11)$$

The new boundary set of any given x_i includes:

$$\mathcal{B}(x_i) = \{x_{j=1..n} \in X \,|\mathcal{N}_{x_i}(x_j) \in [0, 1]\} \quad (12)$$

In the experiments, we tested our RLN approach (9), $0 < \mathcal{N}_{x_i}(x_j) < 1$ for boundary detection, in comparison to the static neighborhood assignments where the number of neighbors, k is fixed.

(3) Graph Formation: Instead of measuring pairwise relations as in (3), we use neighborhood information to represent $\mathcal{G}$. In an analogical manner to (Roweis and Saul, 2000), (Wang and Zhang, 2006), for graph sparcification, for our *Relaxed Linear Neighborhood*, we re-construct each node using a linear combination of its dynamic neighbors:

$$\begin{array}{l} \min_w \sum_i \left\| x_i - \sum_{j: x_j \in \mathcal{B}(x_i)} \mathcal{N}_{x_i}(x_j) w_{ij} x_j \right\|^2 \\ s.t. \sum_j w_{ij} = 1, w_{ij} \geq 0 \end{array} \quad (13)$$

where $0 < \mathcal{N}_{x_i}(x_j) < 1$ is the degree of neighborhood to boundary set $\mathcal{B}(x_i)$ and w_{ij} is degree of contribution of x_j to x_i, to be predicted. A $\mathcal{N}_{x_i}(x_j) = 0$ means no edge link. To prevent negative weights, and satisfy their normalization to unity, we used a constraint in (13) for RLN.

Edge weights of $\mathcal{G}$ are found using above relaxed boundary assumption, and relaxed neighborhood method. A sparse relaxed weight matrix $(\tilde{\mathcal{W}})_{ij} = \tilde{w}_{ij}$ is formed representing different number of connected edges for every node, which are weighted according to their neighborhood density. Since w_{ij} is constructed via linear combination of varying number of neighbors of each node, $\tilde{\mathcal{W}}$ is used as the edge weights of $\mathcal{G}$. Next we form a regularization framework in place of label propagation (LP).

6 Regularization and Inference

Given a set of token-label assignments $\mathcal{X} = \{x_1, ..., x_l, x_{l+1}, ..., x_n\}$, and binary labels of first l points, $\mathcal{Y} = \{y_1, ..., y_l, 0, .., 0\}$, the goal is to predict if the label assignment of any token of a given test question is true or false. Let $\mathcal{F}$ denote set of classifying functions defined on $\mathcal{X}$, and $\forall \mathbf{f} \in \mathcal{F}$ a real value f_i to every point x_i is assigned. At each iteration, any given data point exploits a part of label information from its neighbors, which is determined by RLN. Thus, predicted label of a node x_i at t+1:

$$f_i^{t+1} = \lambda y_i + (1-\lambda) \sum_j \mathcal{N}_{x_i}(x_j) w_{ij} f_j^t \quad (14)$$

where $x_j \in \mathcal{B}x_i$, 0< λ <1 sets a portion of label information that x_i gets from its local neighbors, $\mathbf{f}^t = (f_1^t, f_2^t, ..., f_n^t)$ is the prediction label vector at iteration t and $f^0 = y$. We can re-state (14) as:

$$\mathbf{f}^{t+1} = \lambda y_i + (1-\lambda) \tilde{\mathcal{W}} \mathbf{f}^t \quad (15)$$

Each node's label is updated via (15) until convergence, which might be at $t \rightarrow \infty$. In place of LP, we can develop a regularization framework (Zhou et al., 2004) to learn $\mathbf{f}$. In graph-based SSL, a function over a graph is estimated to satisfy two conditions: (*i*) close to the observed labels , and (*ii*) be smooth on the whole graph via following loss function:

$$\begin{aligned} arg \min \mathcal{Q}(f) = \textstyle\sum_{i=1}^n (f_i - y_i)^2 + \\ \lambda \textstyle\sum_{i,j=1}^n \sum_{j:x_j \in \mathcal{B}(x_i)} \phi_{x_i}(x_j) \langle f_i, f_j \rangle \end{aligned} \quad (16)$$

where $\phi_{x_i}(x_j) = \mathcal{N}_{x_i}(x_j) \tilde{w}_{ij}$. Setting gradient of loss function $\mathcal{Q}(f)$ to zero, we obtain:

$$\partial_f \mathcal{Q}(f) = 2(\mathcal{Y} - \mathbf{f}) + \lambda[(\mathcal{I} - \Phi) + (\mathcal{I} - \Phi)^T]\mathbf{f} \quad (17)$$

Relaxed weight matrix $\tilde{\mathcal{W}}$ is normalized according to constraint in (13), so as degree matrix, $\mathcal{D} = \sum_j \tilde{\mathcal{W}}_{ij}$, and graph Laplacian, i.e., $\mathcal{L} = (\tilde{\mathcal{D}} - \tilde{\mathcal{W}})/\tilde{\mathcal{D}} = \mathcal{I} - \tilde{\mathcal{W}}$. Since f is a function on the manifold and the graph is discretized form of a manifold (Belkin and Niyogi, 2002a), $\mathbf{f}$ can also be regarded as the discrete form of f, which is equivalent at the nodes of graph. So the second term of (16) yields:

$$[(\mathcal{I} - \tilde{\mathcal{W}}) + (\mathcal{I} - \tilde{\mathcal{W}})^T]\mathbf{f} \approx 2\mathcal{L}f \approx [(\mathcal{I} - \tilde{\mathcal{W}})]\mathbf{f} \quad (18)$$

Hence optimum f^* is obtained by new form of derivative in (17) after replacing (18):

$$f^* = (1-\lambda)\left(\mathcal{I} - \lambda\tilde{\mathcal{W}}\right)^{-1} \mathcal{Y} \quad (19)$$

Most graph-based SSLs are transductive, i.e., not easily expendable to new testing points. In (Delalleau et al., 2005) an induction scheme is proposed to classify a new point x_{Te} by

$$\hat{f}(x_{Te}) = \textstyle\sum_{i \in L \cup U} \tilde{\mathcal{W}}_{x_i} f_i / \sum_{i \in L \cup U} \tilde{\mathcal{W}}_{x_i} \quad (20)$$

Thus, we use induction, where we can, to avoid reconstruction of the graph for new test points.

7 Experiments and Discussions

In the next, we evaluate the performance of the proposed RLN in comparison to the other methods on syntactic and real datasets.

Exp. 1. Graph Construction Performance: Here we use a similar syntactic data in (Jebara et al., 2009) shown in Fig.2.a, which contains two clusters of dissimilar densities and shapes. We investigate three graph construction methods, linear k-neighborhoods of (Roweis and Saul, 2000) in Fig.2.b, b-matching(Jebara et al., 2009) in Fig.2.c and RLN of this work in Fig.2.d using a dataset of 300 points with binary output values. b-matching permits a given datum to select k neighboring points but also ensures that exactly k points selects given datum as their neighbor.

In each graph construction method Gaussian kernel distance is used. Experiments are run 50 times where at each fold only 2 labeled samples from opposite classes are used to predict the rest. The experiments are repeated for different *k*, *b* and ϵ values. In Fig. 2, average of trials is shown when *k*, *b* are 10 and ϵ >*0.5*. We also used the ϵN approach but it did not show any improvement over *k*NN approach.

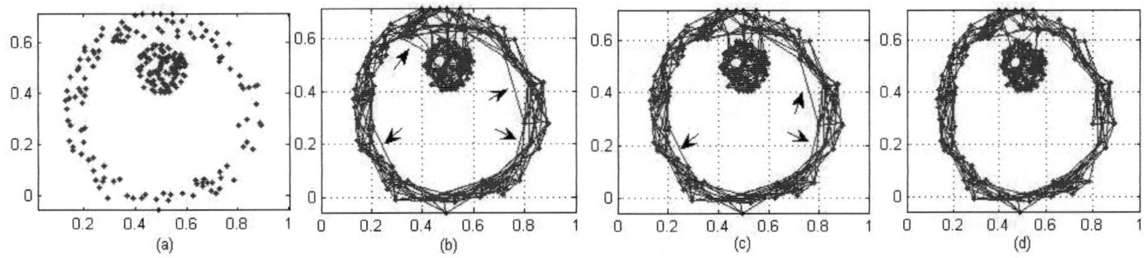

Figure 2: Graph Construction Experiments. (a) Syntactic data. (b) linear k-neighborhood (c) b-matching (d) RLN.

In Fig. 2.d, RLN can separate two classes more efficiently than the rest. Compared to the b-matching approach, RLN clearly improves the robustness. There are more links between clusters in other graph methods than RLN, which shows that RLN can separate two classes much efficiently. Also since dynamic number of edges are constructed with RLN, unnecessary links are avoided, but for the rest of the graph methods there are edges between far away nodes (shown with arrows). In the rest of the experiments, we use b-matching for benchmark as it is the closest approach to the proposed RLN.

Exp. 2. Semantic Component Recognition: We demonstrate the performance of the new RLN with two sets of experiments for sequence labeling of question recognition task. As a first step in understanding semantic components of questions, we asked two annotators to annotate a random subsample of 4000 TREC factoid and description questions obtained from tasks of 1999-2006. There are 11 predefined semantic categories (section 3), close to 280K labeled tokens. Annotators are told that each question must have one topic and zero or one focus and event, zero or more of the rest of the components. Inter-tagger agreement is $\kappa = 0.68$, which denotes a considerable agreement.

We trained models on 3500 random set of questions and reserved the rest of 500 for testing the performance. We applied pre-processing and feature selection of section 3 to compile labeled and unlabeled training and labeled testing datasets. At training time, we performed manual iterative parameter optimization based on prediction accuracy to find the best parameter sets, i.e., $k = \{3, 5, 10, 20, 50\}$, $\epsilon \in \{0, 1\}$, distance = $\{linear, gaussion\}$.

We use the average loss ($\bar{L}$) per sequence (query)

	other	*topic*	*focus*	*event*	*rest*
# Samples	1997	1142	525	264	217
CRF	0.935	0.903	0.823	0.894	0.198
b-matching	0.871	0.900	0.711	0.847	0.174
RLN	0.911	0.910	0.761	0.834	0.180

Table 2: Chunking accuracy on testing data. *'other'*=O, *'topic'*=BT+IT, *'focus'* = BF+IF, *'event'*= 'BE+IE", *'rest'*= rest of the labels, i.e., IE, BC, IC, BCL, ICL.

to evaluate the semantic chunking performance:

$$\bar{L} = \frac{1}{N}\sum_{i=1}^{N}\left[\frac{1}{L_i}\sum_{j=1}^{L_i}\mathcal{I}\left((\hat{y}_i)_j \neq (y_i)_j\right)\right] \quad (21)$$

where $\hat{y}$ and y are predicted and actual sequence respectively; N is the number of test examples; L_i is the length of ith sequence; $\mathcal{I}$ is the 0-1 loss function.

(1) *Chunking Performance:* Here, we investigate the accuracy of our models on individual component prediction. We use CRF, b-matching and our RLN to learn models from labeled training data and evaluate performance on testing dataset. For RLN and b-matching we use training as labeled and testing as unlabeled dataset in transductive way to predict token labels. The testing results are shown in Table 2 for different group of components. The accuracy for 'topic' and 'focus' components are relatively high compared to other components. Most of the errors on the 'rest' labels are due to confusion with 'topic' or 'focus'. On some components, i.e., *topic*, *other*, RLN performed significantly better than b-matching based on t-test statistics (at 95% confidence). No statistical significance between CRF and RLN is observed indicating that RLN's good performance on individual label scoring, as it shows that RLN can be used efficiently for sequence labeling.

(2) *Question Labeling Performance.* Having

Labeled	CRF	SSL	sCRF	b-match	RLN
1%	0.240	0.235	0.223	0.233	**0.220**
5%	0.222	0.218	0.215	0.203	**0.189**
10%	0.170	0.219	0.186	0.194	0.180
25%	0.173	0.196	0.175	0.174	**0.170**
50%	0.160	0.158	0.147	0.156	0.158
75%	0.140	0.163	0.138	0.160	0.155
100%	0.120	0.170	0.123	0.155	0.149

Table 3: Test Data Average Loss on graph construction with RLN, b-matching, standard SSL with kNN as well as CRF, CRF with Self Learning (sCRF).

demonstrated that RLN is an alternative method to the standard sequence learning methods for the question labeling task, next we evaluate per sequence (question) performance, rather than individual label performance using unlabeled data. Firstly, we randomly select subset of labeled training dataset, $X_L^i \subset X_L$ with different sample sizes, $n_L^i = 5\% * n_L$, $10\% * n_L$, $25\% * n_L$, $50\% * n_L$, $75\% * n_L$, $100\% * n_L$, where n_L is the size of X_L. Thus, instead of fixing the number of labeled records and varying the number of unlabeled points, we propose to fix the percentage of unlabeled points in training dataset. We hypothetically use unselected part of the labeled dataset as unlabeled data at each random selection. We compare the result of RLN to other graph based methods including standard SSL (Zhu et al., 2003) using kNN, and b-matching. We also build a CRF model using the same features as RLN except the output information, which CRF learns through probabilistic structure. In addition, we implemente self training for CRF (sCRF), most commonly known SSL method, by adding most confident $(x, f(x))$ unlabeled data back to the data and repeat the process 10 times. Table 3 reports average loss of question recognition tasks on testing dataset using these methods.

When the number of labeled data is small ($n_L^i < 25\% n_L$), RLN has better performance compared to the rest (an average of 7% improvement). The SSL and sCRF performance is slightly better than CRF at this stage. As expected, as the percentage of labeled points in training is increased, the CRF outperforms the rest of the models. However, observing no statistical significance between CRF, b-matching and RLN up to 25-50% labeled points indicates RLNs performance on unlabeled datasets. Thus, for sequence labeling, the RLN can be a better alternative to known sequence labeling methods, when manual annotation of the entire dataset is not feasible.

# Unlabeled tokens	25K	50K	75K	100K
Average Loss	0.150	0.146	0.141	0.139

Table 4: Average Loss Results for RLN graph based SSL as unlabeled tokens is increased.

Exp. 3. Unlabeled Data Performance: Here we evaluate the effect of the size of unlabeled data on the performance of RLN by gradually increasing the size of unlabeled questions. The assumption is that as more unlabeled data is used, the model would have additional spatial information about token neighbors that would help to improve its generalization performance. We used the questions from the Question and Answer pair dataset distributed by Linguistic Data Consortium for the DARPA GALE project (LDC catalog number: LDC2008E16). We compiled 10K questions, consisting of 100K tokens.

Although the error reduction is small (Table 4), the empirical results indicate that unlabeled data can have positive effect on the performance of the RLN method. As we introduce more unlabeled data, the RLN performance is increased, which indicates that there is a lot to discover from unlabeled questions.

8 Conclusions

In this paper, we presented a graph-based semi-supervised learning method with a new graph construction. Our new graph construction relaxes the neighborhood assumptions yielding robust graphs when the labeled data is sparse, in comparison to previous methods, which set rigid boundaries. The new algorithm is particularly appealing to question semantic component recognition task, namely question understanding, in that in this task we usually deal with very few labeled data and considerably larger unlabeled data. Experiments on question semantic component recognition show that our semi-supervised graph-based method can improve performance by up to 7-10% compared to well-known sequence labeling methods, especially when there are more unlabeled data than the labeled data.

References

A. Alexandrescu and K. Kirchhoff. 2007. Data-driven graph construction for semi-supervised graph-based learning in nlp. In *Proc. of HLT 2007*.

M. Belkin and P. Niyogi. 2002a. Laplacian eigenmaps and spectral techniques for embedding and clustering. In *Advances in Neural Information Processing Systems*.

M. Belkin and P. Niyogi. 2002b. Using manifold structure for partially labeled classification. In *Proc. of NIPS 2002*.

M. Belkin, P. Niyogi, and V. Sindhwani. 2006. A geometric framework for learning from examples. In *Journal of Machine Learning Research*.

J. D. Burger. 2006. Mitre's qanda at trec-15. In *Proc. of the TREC-2006*.

J.Y. Chai and R. Jin. 2004. Discourse structure for context question answering. In *Proc. of HLT-NAACL 2004*.

O. Delalleau, Y. Bengio, and N.L. Roux. 2005. Efficient non-parametric function induction in semi-supervised learning. In *Proc. of AISTAT-2005*.

H. Duan, Cao Y, C.Y. Lin, and Y. Yu. 2008. Searching questions by identifying question topic and question focus. In *Proc. of ACL-08*.

S. Fan, Y. Zhang, W.W.Y. Ng, Xuan Wang, and X. Wang. 2008. Semantic chunk annotation for complex questions using conditional random field. In *Coling 2008: Proc. of Workshop on Knowledge and Reasoning for Answering Questions*.

GD. Forney. 1973. The viterbi algorithm. In *Proc. of IEEE 61(3)*, pages 269–278.

A. Goldberg and X. Zhu. 2009. Keepin' it real: Semi-supervised learning with realistic tuning. In *Proc. of NAACL-09 Workshop on Semi-Supervised Learning for NLP*.

E. Hajicova, P. Sgall, and H. Skoumalova. 1993. Identifying topic and focus by an automatic procedure. In *Proc. of the EACL-1993*.

T. Jebara, J. Wang, and S.F. Chang. 2009. Graph construction and b-matching for semi-supervised learning. In *Proc. of ICML-09*.

Dan Klein and Christopher D. Manning. 2003. Accurate unlexicalized parsing. In *Proceedings of the 41st Meeting of the ACL-2003*, pages 423–430.

J.D. Lafferty, A. McCallum, and F. Pereira. 2001. Conditional random fields: Probabilistic models for segmenting and labeling sequence data. In *Proc. of 18th International Conf. on Machine Learning (ICML'01)*.

M. Maier and U.V. Luxburg. 2008. Influence of graph construction on graph-based clustering measures. In *Proc. of Neural Infor. Proc. Sys. (NIPS 2008)*.

M.-C.D. Marneffe, B. MacCartney, and C.D. Manning. 2006. Generating typed-dependency parsers from phrase structure parsers. In *In LREC2006*.

S.T. Roweis and L.K. Saul. 2000. Nonlinear dimensionality reduction by locally embedding. In *Science*, volume 290, pages 2323–2326.

F. Wang and C. Zhang. 2006. Label propagation through linear neighborhoods. In *Proc. of the ICML-2006*.

Dengyong Zhou, Olivier Bousquet, Thomas N. Lal, Jason Weston, and Bernhard Schölkopf. 2004. Learning with local and global consistency. *Advances in Neural Information Processing Systems*, 16:321–328.

Xiaojin Zhu, John Lafferty, and Zoubin Ghahramani. 2003. *Semi-supervised learning: From Gaussian Fields to Gaussian processes*. Technical Report CMU-CS-03-175, Carnegie Mellon University, Pittsburgh.

Capturing the stars: predicting ratings for service and product reviews

Narendra Gupta, Giuseppe Di Fabbrizio and **Patrick Haffner**
AT&T Labs - Research, Inc.
Florham Park, NJ 07932 - USA
{ngupta,pino,haffner}@research.att.com

Abstract

Bloggers, professional reviewers, and consumers continuously create opinion–rich web reviews about products and services, with the result that textual reviews are now abundant on the web and often convey a useful overall rating (number of stars). However, an overall rating cannot express the multiple or conflicting opinions that might be contained in the text, or explicitly rate the different aspects of the evaluated entity. This work addresses the task of automatically predicting ratings, for given aspects of a textual review, by assigning a numerical score to each evaluated aspect in the reviews. We handle this task as both a regression and a classification modeling problem and explore several combinations of syntactic and semantic features. Our results suggest that classification techniques perform better than ranking modeling when handling evaluative text.

1 Introduction

An abundance of service and products reviews are today available on the Web. Bloggers, professional reviewers, and consumers continuously contribute to this rich content both by providing text reviews and often by assigning useful overall ratings (number of stars) to their overall experience. However, the overall rating that usually accompanies online reviews cannot express the multiple or conflicting opinions that might be contained in the text, or explicitly rate the different aspects of the evaluated entity. For example, a restaurant might receive an overall great evaluation, while the service might be rated below average due to slow and discourteous wait staff. Pinpointing opinions in documents, and the entities being referenced, would provide a finer–grained sentiment analysis and a solid foundation to automatically summarize evaluative text, but such a task becomes even more challenging when applied to a generic domain and with unsupervised methods. Some significant contributions by Hu and Liu (2004), Popescu and Etzioni (2005), and Carenini et al. (2006) illustrate different techniques to find and measure opinion orientation in text documents. Other work in sentiment analysis (often referred as *opinion mining*) has explored several facets of the problem, ranging from predicting binary ratings (e.g., *thumbs up/down*) (Turney, 2002; Pang et al., 2002; Dave et al., 2003; Yu and Hatzivassiloglou, 2003; Pang and Lee, 2004; Yi and Niblack, 2005; Carenini et al., 2006), to more detailed opinion analysis methods predicting multi–scale ratings (e.g., *number of stars*) (Pang and Lee, 2005; Snyder and Barzilay, 2007; Shimada and Endo, 2008; Okanohara and Tsujii, 2005).

This paper focuses on multi–scale multi–aspect rating prediction for textual reviews. As mentioned before, textual reviews are abundant, but when trying to make a buy decision on a specific product or service, getting sufficient and reliable information can be a daunting and time consuming task. On one hand, a single overall rating does not provide enough information and could be unreliable, if not supported over a large number of independent reviews/ratings. From another standpoint, reading through a large number of textual reviews in order to infer the aspect ratings could be quite time con-

Proceedings of the NAACL HLT 2010 Workshop on Semantic Search, pages 36–43,
Los Angeles, California, June 2010.

suming, and, at the same time, the outcome of the evaluation could be biased by the reader's interpretation. In this work, instead of a single overall rating, we propose to provide ratings for multiple aspects of the product/service. For example, in the case of restaurant reviews, we consider ratings for five aspects: *food*, *atmosphere*, *value*, *service* and *overall experience*. In Lu et al. (2009) such aspect ratings are called *rated aspect summaries*, in Shimada and Endo (2008) they have been referred to as *seeing stars* and in Snyder and Barzilay (2007) they are referred to as *multi–aspect ranking*. We use supervised learning methods to train predictive models and use a specific decoding method to optimize the aspect rating assignment to a review.

In the rest of this paper, we overview the previous work in this research area in Section 2. We describe the corpus used in the experiments in Section 3. In Section 4 we present various learning algorithms we experimented with. Section 5 explains our experimental setup, while in Section 6 we provide analysis of our experimental results. Section 7 presents details of modeling and exploiting interdependence among aspect ratings to boost the predictive performance. Finally, we describe the future work in Section 8 and report the concluding remarks in Section 9.

2 Related work

Previous work in sentiment analysis (Turney, 2002; Pang et al., 2002; Dave et al., 2003; Yu and Hatzivassiloglou, 2003; Pang and Lee, 2004; Yi and Niblack, 2005; Carenini et al., 2006) used different information extraction and supervised classification methods to detect document opinion polarity (positive vs. negative).

By conducting a limited experiment with two subjects, Pang and Lee (2005) demonstrated that humans can discern more grades of positive or negative judgments by accurately detecting small differences in rating scores by just looking at review text. In a five–star schema, for instance, the subjects were able to perfectly distinguish rating differences of three *notches* or 1.5 stars and correctly perceive differences of one star with an average of 83% accuracy. This insight confirms that a five–star scale improves the evaluative information and is perceived with the right discriminative strength by the users.

Pang and Lee applied supervised and semi–supervised classification techniques, in addition to *linear,* ϵ*-insensitive* SVM regression methods, to predict the overall ratings of movie reviews in three and four–class star rating schemes. In the books review domain, Okanohara and Tsujii (2005) show a similar approach with comparable results. Both these contributions consider only overall ratings, which could be sufficient to describe sentiment for movie and book reviews. Two recent endeavors, Snyder and Barzilay (2007) for the restaurants domain, and Shimada and Endo (2008) for video games reviews, exploit multi–aspect, multiple rating modeling. Snyder and Barzilay (2007) assume inter–dependencies among the aspect ratings and capture the relationship between the ratings via the *agreement relation*. The agreement relation describes the likelihood that the user will express the same rating for all the rated aspects. Interestingly, Snyder and Barzilay (2007) show that modeling aspect rating dependencies helps to reduce the rank loss by keeping in consideration the contributions of the opinion strength of the single aspects referred to in the review. They incorporated information about the aspect rating dependencies in a regression model and minimized the loss (overall *grief*) during decoding. Shimada and Endo (2008) exploits a more traditional supervised machine learning approach where features such as word unigrams and frequency counts are used to train classification and regression models. As detailed in Section 4, our approach is similar to (Snyder and Barzilay, 2007) in terms of review domain and algorithms, but we improve on their performances by optimizing classification predictions.

3 Reviews corpus

Labeled data containing textual reviews and aspect ratings are rarely available. For this work, reviews were mined from the `we8there.com` websites around the end of 2008. `we8there.com` is one of the few websites, where, besides textual reviews, numerical ratings for different aspects of restaurants are also provided. Aspects used for rating on this site are: *food*, *service*, *atmosphere*, *value* and *overall experience*. Ratings are given on a scale from 1 to 5; for example, reviewers posting opinions were asked to rank their overall experience by the following prompt: *"On a scale of 1 (poor) to 5 (excellent), please rate your dining experience"*, and then enter a textual description by the prompt: *"Please describe your experience (30 words minimum)"*. At the time of mining, this site had reviews of about 3,800 restaurants with an average of two reviews per restaurant containing around eight sentences per review. A more detailed description is reported in Table 1. Table 2 shows review ratings distribution over the aspects. Rating distributions are evidently skewed toward high ratings with 70% or more reviews appraised as *excellent* (rank 5) or *above average* (rank 4).

Restaurants	3,866
Reviewers	4,660
Reviews	6,823
Average reviews per restaurant	1.76
Number of sentences	58,031
Average sentences per review	8.51

Table 1: Restaurant review corpus

Rating	1	2	3	4	5
Atmosphere	6.96	7.81	14.36	23.70	47.18
Food	8.24	6.72	9.86	18.53	56.65
Value	9.37	7.57	13.61	23.27	46.18
Service	11.83	6.12	11.91	22.00	48.14
Overall	10.48	8.19	10.17	20.47	50.69

Table 2: Restaurant review ratings distribution per aspect

4 Learning algorithms

In this section we review machine learning approaches that can predict ordinal ratings from textual data. The goal is *ordinal regression*, which differs from traditional numeric regression because the targets belong to a discrete space, but also differs from classification as one wants to minimize the rank loss rather than the classification error. The rank loss is the average difference between actual and predicted ratings and is defined as

$$\mathit{RankLoss} = \frac{1}{N}\sum_{i}^{N}(|r_{a_i} - r_{p_i}|)$$

where r_{a_i} and r_{p_i} are actual and predicted ratings respectively for the instance i, and N is the number of considered reviews. There are several possible approaches to such a regression problem.

1. The most obvious approach is *numeric regression*. It is implemented with a neural network trained using the back–propagation algorithm.
2. Ordinal regression can also be implemented with *multiple thresholds* ($r - 1$ thresholds are used to split r ranks). This is implemented with a Perceptron based ranking model called *PRank* (Crammer and Singer, 2001).
3. Since rating aspects with values 1, 2, 3, 4 and 5 is an ordinal regression problem it can also be interpreted as a *classification* problem, with one class per possible rank. In this interpretation, ordering information is not directly used to help classification. Our implementation uses binary one-vs-all Maximum Entropy (MaxEnt) classifiers. We will see that this very simple approach can be extended to handle aspect interdependency, as presented in section 7.

In order to provide us with a broad range of rating prediction strategies, we experimented with a numerical regression technique viz. neural network, an ordinal regression technique viz. PRank algorithm, and a classification technique viz. MaxEnt classifiers. Their implementations are straightforward and the run–time highly efficient. After selecting a strategy from the previous list, one could consider more advanced algorithms described in Section 8.

5 Experimental setup

To predict aspect ratings of restaurants from their textual reviews we used the reviews mined from the `we8there.com` website to train different regression and classification models as outlined in Section 4. In each of our experiments, we randomly partitioned the data into 90% for training and 10% for testing. This ensures that the distributions in training and test data are identical. All the results quoted in this paper are averages of 10–fold cross–validation over 6,823 review examples. We conducted repeatedly the same experiment on 10 different training/test partitions and computed the average rank loss over all the test partitions.

Figure 1 illustrates the training process where each aspect is described by a separate predictive model.

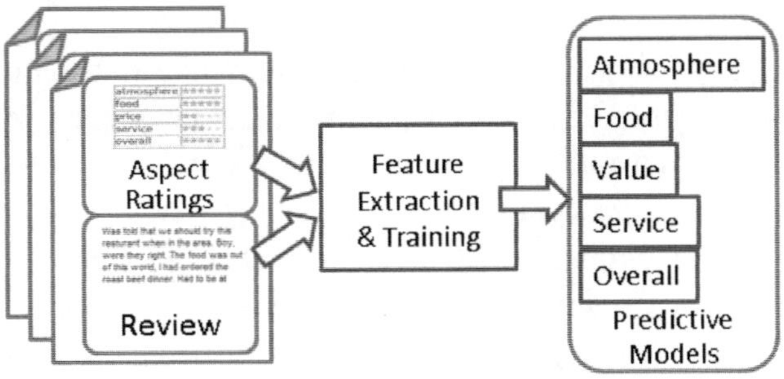

Figure 1: Predictive model training

We introduce the following notation that will be helpful in further discussion. There are m aspects. For our data m is 5. Each aspect can have an integer rating from 1 to k. Once again, for our data k is 5. Each review text document t can have ratings $\mathbf{r}$, which is a vector of m integers ranging 1 to k (bold faced letters indicate vectors). Using the training data $(t_1, \mathbf{r}^1)..(t_i, \mathbf{r}^i)..(t_n, \mathbf{r}^n)$ we train m *rating predictors* $R_j(t_i)$, one for each aspect j. Given text t_i predictor R_j outputs the most likely rating l for the aspect j. In these experiments, we treated aspect rating predictors as independent of each other. For each rated aspect, predictor models were trained independently and were used independently to predict ratings for each aspect.

5.1 Feature Selection

We experimented with different combinations of features, including word unigrams, bigrams, *word chunks*, and *parts–of–speech* (POS) chunks. The assumption is that bag–of–unigrams capture the basic word statistic and that bigrams take into account some limited word context. POS chunks and word chunks discriminate the use of words in the context (e.g., a simple form word sense disambiguation) and, at the same time, aggregate co–occurring words (e.g., collocations), such as *sautéed_onions*, *buffalo_burger*, etc.

Most of the web–based reviews do not usually provide fine–grained aspect ratings of products or services, however, they often give an overall rating evaluation. We therefore also experimented with the overall rating as an input feature to predict the more specific aspect ratings. Results of our experiments are shown in Table 3.

Aspects	Uni-gram	Bi-gram	Word Chunks	Word Chunks POS Chunks	Uni gram Overall Rating
Atmosphere	0.740	0.763	0.789	0.783	0.527
Food	0.567	0.571	0.596	0.588	0.311
Value	0.703	0.725	0.751	0.743	0.406
Service	0.627	0.640	0.651	0.653	0.377
overall	0.548	0.559	0.577	0.583	
Average	0.637	0.652	0.673	0.670	0.405

Table 3: Average ranking losses using MaxEnt classifier with different feature sets

Review sentences
<s>Poor service made the lunch unpleasant.</s> <s>The staff was unapologetic about their mistakes they just didn't seem to care.</s> <s>For example the buffalo burger I ordered with sauteed onions and fries initially was served without either.</s> <s> The waitress said she'd bring out the onions but had I waited for them before eating the burger the meat would have been cold.</s> <s>Other examples of the poor service were that the waitress forgot to bring out my soup when she brought out my friend's salad and we had to repeatedly ask to get our water glasses refilled.</s> <s> When asked how our meal was I did politely mention my dissatisfaction with the service but the staff person's response was silence not even a simple I m sorry.</s> <s>I won't return. </s>
Word Chunks
poor_service made lunch unpleasant staff unapologetic mistakes n't care example buffalo_burger ordered sauteed_onions fries served waitress said bring onions waited eating burger meat cold other_examples poor_service waitress_forgot bring soup brought friend salad repeatedly ask_to_get water glasses_refilled asked meal politely_mention dissatisfaction service staff_person response silence not simple sorry n't return
Parts-of-speech Chunks
NNP_NN VBD NN JJ NN JJ NNS RB VB NN NN_NN VBD NN_NNS NNS VBN NN VBD VB NNS VBD VBG NN NN JJ JJ_NNS JJ_NN NN_NN VB NN VBD NN NN RB VB_TO_VB NN VBZ_VBN VBD NN RB_VB NN NN NN_NN NN NN RB JJ JJ RB VB

Table 4: Example of reviews and extracted word chunks

Unigram and bigram features refer to unigram words and bigram words occurring more than 3 times in the training corpus. Word chunks are obtained by only processing Noun (NP), Verb (VP) and Adjective (ADJP) phrases in the review text. We removed modals and auxiliary verbs form VPs, pronouns from NPs and we broke the chunks containing conjunctions. Table 4 shows an example of extracted word and parts–of–speech chunks from review text. As can be seen, word chunks largely keep the information bearing chunks phrases and remove the rest. Parts–of–speech chunks are simply parts–of–speech of word chunks.

In spite of richness of word and parts-of-speech, chunks models using word unigrams perform the best. We can attribute this to the data sparseness, never–the–less, this results is in line with the findings in Pang et al. (2002). Last column of Table 3 clearly shows that use of overall rating as input feature significantly improves the performance. Clearly this validates the intuition that aspect ratings are highly co–related with overall ratings.

For the remaining experiments, we used only the unigram words as features of the review text. Since overall ratings given by reviewers may contain their biases and since they may not always be available, we did not use them as input features. Our hope is that even though we train the predictors using reviewers provided aspect ratings, learned models will be able to predict aspect ratings that depend only on the review text and not on reviewer's biases.

5.2 Results

Table 5 shows the results of our evaluation. Each row in this table reports average rank loss of four different models for each aspect. The baseline rank loss is computed by setting the predicted rank for all test examples to 5, as it is the most frequently occurring rank in the training data (see also Table 2). As shown in Table 5, the average baseline rank loss is greater than one. The third column shows the results from the neural network–based numeric regression. The fourth column corresponds to the Perceptron–based PRank algorithm. The MaxEnt classification results appear in the last column. For these results, we also detail the standard deviation over the 10 cross–validation trials.

Aspects	Base-line	Back-Prop.	Percep-tron	MaxEnt
Atmosphere	1.036	0.772	0.930	0.740 ± 0.022
Food	0.912	0.618	0.739	0.567 ± 0.033
Value	1.114	0.740	0.867	0.703 ± 0.028
Service	1.116	0.708	0.851	0.627 ± 0.033
Overall	1.077	0.602	0.756	0.548 ± 0.026
Average	1.053	0.694	0.833	0.637 ± 0.020

Table 5: Average ranking losses using different predictive models

6 Analysis

As can be seen in table Table 5, *Atmosphere* and *Value* are the worst performers. This is caused by the missing textual support for these aspects in the training data. Using manual examination of small number of examples, we found that only 62% of user given ratings have supporting text for ratings of these aspects in the reviews.

For example, in Figure 2 the first review clearly expresses opinions about food, service and atmosphere (*under appall of cigarette smoke*), but there is no evidence about *value* which is ranked three, two notches above the other aspects. Similarly, the second review is all about food without any reference to *service* rated two notches above the other aspects, or *atmosphere* or *value*.

Because of this reason, we do not expect any predictive model to do much better than 62% accuracy. Manual examination of a small number of examples also showed that 55% of ratings predicted by MaxEnt models are supported by the review text. This is 89% of 62% (a rough upper bound) and can be considered satisfactory given small data set and differences among reviewers rating preference. One way to boost the predictive performance would be to first determine if there is a textual support for an aspect rating, and use only the supported aspect ratings for training and evaluation of the models. This however, will require labeled data that we tried to avoid in this work.

Aspects	Ratings	Reviews
Atmosphere Food Value Service Overall	★★☆☆☆ ★★☆☆☆ ★★★☆☆ ★★☆☆☆ ★★☆☆☆	Heavy, uninspired food, eaten under appall of cigarette smoke. Very slow service, though not unfriendly. There are many better restaurants in Ashland. Not recommended.
Atmosphere Food Value Service Overall	★★★☆☆ ★★★☆☆ ★★★☆☆ ★★★★☆ ★★★☆☆	I'll have to disagree with Ms. Kitago's take on at least one part of the evening. I believe the chicken Tikka Marsala was slightly dry. Decent portion, but not succulent as i am accustomed to. In addition, the Gulub Jaman is served cold, anathema to this diner. I will agree with Ms. K that the mango lassi was delicious, but overall I believe her review was slightly inflated

Figure 2: Example of ratings with partial support in the text review

To our surprise, MaxEnt classification, although it minimizes a classification error, performs best even when evaluated using rank loss. As can be noticed, the performance difference over the second best approach (back–propagation) usually exceeds the standard deviation.

MaxEnt results are also comparable to those presented in Snyder and Barzilay (2007) using the *Good Grief* algorithm. Snyder and Barzilay (2007) also used data from the `we8there.com` website. While we are using the same data source, note the following differences: (i) Snyder and Barzilay (2007) used only 4,488 reviews as opposed to the 6,823 reviews used in our work; (ii) our results are averaged over a 10 fold cross validation. As shown with the baseline results reported in Table 6, the impact on performance that can be attributed to these differences is small. The most significant number, which should minimize the impact of data discrepancy, is the improvement over baseline (labeled as *"gain over baseline"* in Table 6). In that respect, our MaxEnt classification–based approach outperforms *Good Grief* for every aspect. Note also that, while we trained 5 independent predictors (one for each aspect) using only word unigrams as features, the *Good Grief* algorithm additionally modeled the agreements among aspect ratings and used the presence/absence of opposing polarity words in reviews as additional features.

	Our results			Snyder and Barzilay (2007)		
Aspects	Base-line	Max Ent.	Gain over Base-line	Base-line	Good Grief	Gain over Base-line
Atmosphere	1.039	0.740	0.299	1.044	0.774	0.270
Food	0.912	0.567	0.344	0.848	0.534	0.314
Value	1.114	0.703	0.411	1.030	0.644	0.386
Service	1.116	0.627	0.489	1.056	0.622	0.434
Overall	1.077	0.548	0.529	1.028	0.632	0.396

Table 6: Comparison of rank loss obtained from MaxEnt classification and those reported in Snyder and Barzilay (2007)

7 Modeling interdependence among aspect ratings

Inspired by these observations, we also trained MaxEnt classifiers to predict pair–wise absolute differences in aspect ratings. Since the difference in ratings of any two aspects can only be 0,1,2,3 or 4, there are 5 classes to predict. For each test example, MaxEnt classifiers output the posterior probability to observe a class given an input example. In our approach, we use these probabilities to compute the best joint assignment of ratings to all aspects. More specifically, in our modified algorithm we use 2 types of classifiers.

- **Rating predictors** - Given the text t_i, our classifiers $R_j(t_i)$ output vectors $\mathbf{p}^i$ consisting of probabilities p^i_l for text t_i having a rating l for the aspect j.
- **Difference predictors** - These correspond to classifiers $D_{j,k}(t_i)$ which output vectors $\mathbf{p}^{i_{j,k}}$. Elements of these vectors are the probabilities that the difference between ratings of aspects j and k is 0,1,2,3 and 4, respectively. While j ranges from 1 to m, k ranges from 1 to $j-1$. Thus, we trained a total of $m(m-1)/2 = 10$ difference predictors.

To predict aspect ratings for a given review text t_i we use both rating predictors and difference predictors and generate output probabilities. We then select the most likely values of $\mathbf{r}^i$ for text t_i that satisfies the probabilistic constraints generated by the predictors. More specifically:

$$\mathbf{r}_i = \underset{\mathbf{r}\in\mathfrak{R}}{argmax} \sum_{j=1}^{m} log(p^i_{r_j}) + \sum_{j=1}^{m}\sum_{k=1}^{j} log(p^{i_{j,k}}_{|r_j - r_k|})$$

$\mathfrak{R}$ is the set of all possible ratings assignments to all aspects. In our case it contains 5^5 (3,125) tuples. tuples in our case. Like Snyder and Barzilay (2007), we also experimented with additional features indicating presence of positive and negative polarity words in the review text. Besides unigrams in the review text, we also used 3 features: the counts of positive and negative polarity words and their differences. Polarity labels are obtained from a dictionary of about 700 words. This dictionary was created by first collecting words used as adjectives in a corpus of un–related review text. We then retained only those words in the dictionary that, in a context free manner generally conveyed positive or negative evaluation of any object, event or situation. Some examples of negative words are *awful, bad, boring, crude, disappointing, horrible, worst, worthless, yucky* and some examples of positive words are *amazing, beautiful, delightful, good, impeccable, lovable, marvelous, pleasant, recommendable, sophisticated, superb, wonderful, wow*. Table 7 first shows gains obtained from using difference predictors, and then gains from using polarity word features in addition to these difference predictors.

Aspects	MaxEnt	+ Difference predictor	+ Polarity features
Atmosphere	0.740	0.718	0.707
Food	0.567	0.552	0.547
Value	0.703	0.695	0.685
Service	0.627	0.627	0.617
Overall	0.548	0.547	0.528
Average	0.637	0.628	0.617

Table 7: Improved rank loss obtained by using difference predictors and polarity word features

8 Future Work

We have presented 3 algorithms chosen for their simplicity of implementation and run time efficiency. The results suggest that our classification–based approach performs better than numeric or ordinal regression approaches. Our next step is to verify these results with the more advanced algorithms outlined below.

1. For many numeric regression problems, (boosted) classification trees have shown good performance.

2. Several multi–threshold implementations of Support Vector Ordinal Regression are compared in Chu and Keerthi (2005). While they are more principled than the Perceptron–based PRank, their implementation is significantly more complex. A simpler approach that performs regression using a single classifier extracts extended examples from the original examples (Li and Lin, 2007).

3. Among classification–based approaches, nested binary classifiers have been proposed (Frank and Hall, 2001) to take into account the ordering information, but the prediction procedure based on classifier score difference is ad–hoc.

9 Conclusions

Textual reviews for different products and services are abundant. Still, when trying to make a buy decision, getting sufficient and reliable information can be a daunting task. In this work, instead of a single overall rating we focus on providing ratings for multiple aspects of the product/service. Since most textual reviews are rarely accompanied by multiple aspect ratings, such ratings must be deduced from predictive models. Several authors in the past have studied this problem using both classification and regression models. In this work we show that even though the aspect rating problem seems like a regression problem, maximum entropy classification models perform the best. Results also show a strong inter–dependence in the way users rate different aspects.

Acknowledgments

We thank Remi Zajac and his team for their support.

References

Carenini, Giuseppe, Raymond T. Ng, and Adam Pauls. 2006. Interactive multimedia summaries of evaluative text. In *Proceedings of Intelligent User Interfaces (IUI)*. ACM Press, pages 124–131.

Chu, Wei and S. Sathiya Keerthi. 2005. New approaches to support vector ordinal regression. In *Proceedings of the 22nd International Conference on Machine Learning*. Bonn, Germany, pages 145–152.

Crammer, Koby and Yoram Singer. 2001. Pranking with ranking. In *Advances in Neural Information Processing Systems 14*. MIT Press, pages 641–647.

Dave, Kushal, Steve Lawrence, and David M. Pennock. 2003. Mining the peanut gallery: Opinion extraction and semantic classification of product reviews. In *WWW '03: Proceedings of the 12th International Conference on World Wide Web*. ACM, New York, NY, USA, pages 519–528.

Frank, Eibe and Mark Hall. 2001. A simple approach to ordinal classification. In *Proceedings of the Twelfth European Conference on Machine Learning*. Springer-Verlag, Berlin, pages 145–156.

Hu, Minqing and Bing Liu. 2004. Mining and summarizing customer reviews. In *KDD '04: Proceedings of the 10th ACM SIGKDD International Conference on Knowledge Discovery and Data Mining*. ACM, New York, NY, USA, pages 168–177.

Li, Ling and Hsuan-Tien Lin. 2007. Ordinal regression by extended binary classification. In B. Schölkopf, J. C. Platt, and T. Hofmann, editors, *Advances in Neural Information Processing Systems 19*. MIT Press, pages 865–872.

Lu, Yue, ChengXiang Zhai, and Neel Sundaresan. 2009. Rated aspect summarization of short comments. In *WWW '09: Proceedings of the 18th International Conference on World Wide Web*. ACM, New York, NY, USA, pages 131–140.

Okanohara, Daisuke and Jun-ichi Tsujii. 2005. Assigning polarity scores to reviews using machine learning techniques. In Robert Dale, Kam-Fai Wong, Jian Su, and Oi Yee Kwong, editors, *IJCNLP*. Springer, volume 3651 of *Lecture Notes in Computer Science*, pages 314–325.

Pang, Bo and Lillian Lee. 2004. A sentimental education: Sentiment analysis using subjectivity summarization based on minimum cuts. In *Proceedings of the Association for Computational Linguistics (ACL)*. pages 271–278.

Pang, Bo and Lillian Lee. 2005. Seeing stars: Exploiting class relationships for sentiment categorization with respect to rating scales. In *Proceedings of the Association for Computational Linguistics (ACL)*. pages 115–124.

Pang, Bo, Lillian Lee, and Shivakumar Vaithyanathan. 2002. Thumbs up? Sentiment classification using machine learning techniques. In *Proceedings of the Conference on Empirical Methods in Natural Language Processing (EMNLP)*. pages 79–86.

Popescu, Ana-Maria and Oren Etzioni. 2005. Extracting product features and opinions from reviews. In *Proceedings of the Human Language Technology Conference and the Conference on Empirical Methods in Natural Language Processing (HLT/EMNLP)*.

Shimada, Kazutaka and Tsutomu Endo. 2008. Seeing several stars: A rating inference task for a document containing several evaluation criteria. In *Advances in Knowledge Discovery and Data Mining, 12th Pacific-Asia Conference, PAKDD 2008*. Springer, Osaka, Japan, volume 5012 of *Lecture Notes in Computer Science*, pages 1006–1014.

Snyder, Benjamin and Regina Barzilay. 2007. Multiple aspect ranking using the Good Grief algorithm. In *Proceedings of the Joint Human Language Technology/North American Chapter of the ACL Conference (HLT-NAACL)*. pages 300–307.

Turney, Peter. 2002. Thumbs up or thumbs down? Semantic orientation applied to unsupervised classification of reviews. In *Proceedings of the Association for Computational Linguistics (ACL)*. pages 417–424.

Yi, Jeonghee and Wayne Niblack. 2005. Sentiment mining in WebFountain. In *Proceedings of the International Conference on Data Engineering (ICDE)*.

Yu, Hong and Vasileios Hatzivassiloglou. 2003. Towards answering opinion questions: Separating facts from opinions and identifying the polarity of opinion sentences. In *Proceedings of the Conference on Empirical Methods in Natural Language Processing (EMNLP)*.

Object Search: Supporting Structured Queries in Web Search Engines

Kim Cuong Pham[†], **Nicholas Rizzolo**[†], **Kevin Small**[‡], **Kevin Chen-Chuan Chang**[†], **Dan Roth**[†]

University of Illinois at Urbana-Champaign[†]
Department of Computer Science
{kimpham2, rizzolo, kcchang, danr}@illinois.edu

Tufts University[‡]
Department of Computer Science
kevin.small@tufts.edu

Abstract

As the web evolves, increasing quantities of structured information is embedded in web pages in disparate formats. For example, a digital camera's description may include its *price* and *megapixels* whereas a professor's description may include her *name*, *university*, and *research interests*. Both types of pages may include additional ambiguous information. General search engines (GSEs) do not support queries over these types of data because they ignore the web document semantics. Conversely, describing requisite semantics through structured queries into databases populated by information extraction (IE) techniques are expensive and not easily adaptable to new domains. This paper describes a methodology for rapidly developing search engines capable of answering structured queries over unstructured corpora by utilizing machine learning to avoid explicit IE. We empirically show that with minimum additional human effort, our system outperforms a GSE with respect to structured queries with clear object semantics.

1 Introduction

General search engines (GSEs) are sufficient for fulfilling the information needs of most queries. However, they are often inadequate for retrieving web pages that concisely describe real world objects as these queries require analysis of both unstructured text and structured data contained in web pages. For example, digital cameras with specific *brand*, *megapixel*, *zoom*, and *price* attributes might be found on an online shopping website, or a professor with her *name*, *university*, *department*, and *research interest* attributes might be found on her homepage. Correspondingly, as the web continues to evolve from a general text corpus into a heterogeneous collection of documents, targeted retrieval strategies must be developed for satisfying these more precise information needs. We accomplish this by using structured queries to capture the intended semantics of a user query and learning domain specific ranking functions to represent the hidden semantics of object classes contained in web pages.

It is not uncommon for a user to want to pose an *object query* on the web. For example, an online shopper might be looking for *shopping pages* that sell *canon* digital cameras with 5 megapixels costing no more than *$300*. A graduate student might be looking for *homepages* of *computer science* professors who work in the *information retrieval* area. Such users expect to get a list web pages containing objects they are looking for, or *object pages*, which we will define more precisely in later sections.

GSEs rarely return satisfactory results when the user has a structured query in mind for two primary reasons. Firstly, GSEs only handle keyword queries whereas structured queries frequently involve data field semantics (e.g. numerical constraints) and exhibit field interdependencies. Secondly, since GSEs are domain-agnostic, they will generally rank camera pages utilizing the same functions as a professor's homepage, ignoring much of the structured information specific to particular domains.

Conversely, vertical search engines (e.g. DBLife, cazoodle.com, Rexa.info, etc.) approach this prob-

Proceedings of the NAACL HLT 2010 Workshop on Semantic Search, pages 44–52,
Los Angeles, California, June 2010.

lem from the information extraction (IE) perspective. Instead of searching an inverted index directly, they first extract data records from text (Kushmerick et al., 1997; McCallum et al., 2000). IE solutions, even with large scale techniques (Agichtein, 2005), do not scale to the *entire* web and cost significantly more than GSEs. Secondly, creating domain-specific models or wrappers require labeling training examples and human expertise for each individual site. Thirdly, pre-extracting information lacks flexibility; decisions made during IE are irrevocable, and at query time, users may find additional value in partial or noisy records that were discarded by the IE system.

These issues motivate our novel approach for designing a GSE capable of answering complex structured queries, which we refer to as *Object Search*. At a high level, we search web pages containing structured information directly over their feature index, similarly to GSEs, adding expressivity by reformulating the structured query such that it can be executed on a traditional inverted index. Thus, we avoid the expense incurred by IE approaches when supporting new object domains. From a technical perspective, this work describes a principled approach to customizing GSEs to answer structured queries from any domain by proposing a compositional ranking model for ranking web pages with regards to structured queries and presenting an interactive learning approach that eases the process of training for a new domain.

2 The Object Search Problem

The Object Search problem is to find the *object pages* that answer a user's *object query*. An object query belongs to an *object domain*. An object domain defines a set of object attributes. An object query is simply a set of constraints over these attributes. Thus we define an object query as a tuple of n constraints $q \equiv c_1 \wedge c_2 \wedge .. \wedge c_n$, where c_i is a constraint on attribute a_i. More specifically, a constraint c_i is defined as a set of acceptable values θ_i for attribute a_i; i.e. $c_i = (a_i \in \theta_i)$. For example, an equality constraint such as "the brand is Canon" can be specified as $(a_{brand} \in \{Canon\})$ and a numeric range constraint such as "the price is at most $200" can be specified as $(a_{price} \in [0, 200])$. When the user does not care about an attribute, the constraint is the constant $true$.

Given an object query, we want a set of satisfying object pages. Specifically, object pages are pages that represent exactly one inherent object on the web. Pages that list several objects such as a department directory page or camera listing pages are not considered object pages because even though they mentioned the object, they do not represent any particular object. There is often a single object page but there are many web pages that mention the object.

The goal of Object Search is similar to learning to rank problems (Liu, 2009), in that its goal is to learn a ranking function $\rho : \mathcal{D} \times \mathcal{Q} \rightarrow \mathcal{R}$ that ranks any $(document, query)$ pairs. This is accomplished by learning an function over a set of relevant features. Each feature can be modeled as a function that takes the pair and outputs a real value $\phi : \mathcal{D} \times \mathcal{Q} \rightarrow \mathcal{R}$. For example, a *term frequency* feature outputs the number of times the query appears in the document. We define a function $\Phi = (\phi_1, \phi_2, ...\phi_n)$ that takes a $(document, query)$ pair and outputs a vector of features. The original ranking function can be written as $\rho(d, q) = \rho'(\Phi(d, q))$ where $\rho' : \mathcal{R}^n \rightarrow \mathcal{R}$ is the function; i.e.:

$$\rho = \rho' \circ \Phi \tag{1}$$

Despite the similarities, Object Search differs from traditional information retrieval (IR) problems in many respects. First, IR can answer only keyword queries whereas an object query is structured by keyword constraints as well as numeric constraints. Second, Object Search results are "focused", in the sense that they must contain an object, as opposed to the broad notion of *relevance* in IR. Finally, since object pages of different domains might have little in common, we cannot apply the same ranking function for different object domains.

As a consequence, in a learning to rank problem, the set of features Φ are fixed for all query. The major concern is learning the function ρ'. In Object Search settings, we expect different Φ for each object domain. Thus, we have to derive both Φ and ρ'.

There are a number of challenges in solving these problems. First, we need a deeper understanding of structured information embedded in web pages. In many cases, an object attribute such as professor's university might appear only once in his homepage. Thus, using a traditional bag-of-words model is often insufficient, because one cannot distinguish the professor own university from other university mentioned in his homepage. Second, we will need training data to train a new ranking function for each new object domain. Thus, we require an efficient bootstrapping method to tackle this problem. Finally, any acceptable solution must scale to the size of the web. This requirement poses challenges for efficient query processing and efficient ranking via the learned ranking function.

3 Object Search Framework

In this section, we illustrate the primary intuitions behind our aproach for an Object Search solution. We describe its architecture, which serves as a search engine framework to support structured queries of any domain. The technical details of major components are left for subsequent sections.

3.1 Intuition

The main idea behind our proposed approach is that we develop different vertical search engines to support object queries in different domains. However, we want to keep the cost of supporting each new domain as small as possible. The key principles to keep the cost small are to 1) share as much as possible between search engines of different domains and 2) automate the process as much as possible using machine learning techniques. To illustrate our proposed approach, we suppose that an user is searching the web for cameras. Her object query is $q = a_{brand} \in \{canon\} \wedge a_{price} \in [0, 200]$.

First, we have to automatically learn a function ρ that ranks web pages given an object query as described in Section 2. We observe web pages relevant to the query and notice several salient features such as "the word *canon* appears in the title", "the word *canon* appears near *manufacturer*", "interesting words that appear include *powershot, eos, ixus*", and "a price value appears after '\$' near the word *price* or *sale*". Intuitively, pages containing these features have a much higher chance of containing the Canon camera being searched. Given labeled training data, we can learn a ranking function that combines these features to produce the probability of a page containing the desired camera object.

Furthermore, we need to answer user query at query time. We need to be able to look up these features efficiently from our index of the web. A naïve method to index the web is to store a list of web pages that have the above features, and at query time, union all pages that have one or more features, aggregate the score for each web page, and return the ranked result. There are three problems with this method. First, these features are dependent on each object domain; thus, the size of the index will increase as the number of domains grows. Second, each time a new domain is added, a new set of features needs to be indexed, and we have to extract features for every single web page again. Third, we have to know beforehand the list of camera brands, megapixel ranges, price ranges, etc, which is infeasible for most object domain.

However, we observe that the above query dependent features can be computed efficiently from a query independent index. For example, whether "the word *canon* appears near *manufacturer*" can be computed if we index all occurrences of the words *canon* and *manufacturer*. Similarly, the feature "the word *canon* appears in the title" can be computed if we index all the words from web pages' title, which only depends on the web pages themselves. Since the words and numbers from different parts of a web page can be indexed independently of the object domain, we can share them across different domains. Thus, we follow the first principle mentioned above.

Of course, computing query dependent features from the domain independent index is more expensive than computing it from the naïve index above. However, this cost is scalable to the web. As a matter of fact, these features are equivalent to "phrase search" features in modern search engines.

Thus, at a high level, we solve the Object Search problem by learning a domain dependent ranking function for each object domain. We store basic domain independent features of the web in our index. At query time, we compute domain dependent features from this index and apply the ranking function to return a ranked list of web pages. In this paper, we focus on the learning problems, leaving the problem of efficient query processing for future work.

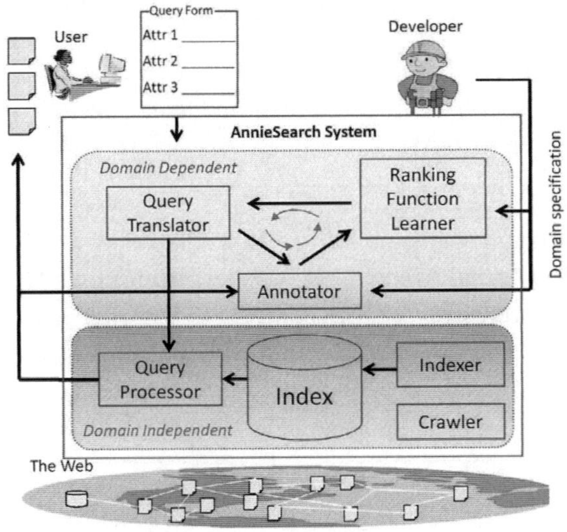

Figure 1: Object Search Architecture

3.2 System Architecture

The main goal of our Object Search system is to enable searching the web with object queries. In order to do this, the system must address the challenges described in Section 2. From the end-user's point of view, the system must promptly and accurately return web pages for their object query. From the developer's point of view, the system must facilitate building a new search engine to support his object domain of interest. The goal of the architecture is to orchestrate all of these requirements.

Figure 1 depicts Object Search architecture. It shows how different components of Object Search interact with an end-user and a developer. The end-user can issue any object query of known domains. Each time the system receives an object query from the end-user, it translates the query into a domain independent feature query. Then the Query Processor executes the feature query on the inverted index, aggregates the features using learned function ρ', and returns a ranked list of web pages to the user.

The developer's job is to define his object domain and train a ranking function for it. He does it by incrementally training the function. He starts by annotating a few web pages and running a learning algorithm to produce a ranking function, which is then used to retrieve more data for the developer to annotate. The process iterates until the developer is satisfied with his trained ranking function for the object domain.

More specifically, the Ranking Function Learner module learns the function ρ' and Φ as mentioned in Section 2. The Query Translator instantiates Φ with user object query q, resulting in $\Phi(q)$. Recall that Φ is a set of feature functions ϕ_i. Each ϕ_i is a function of a (d, q) pair such as "term frequency of a_k in title" (a_k is an attribute of the object). Thus we can instantiate $\phi(q)$ by replacing a_k with θ_k, which is part of the query q. For example, if $\theta_k = \{canon\}$ in the previous example, then $\phi(q)$ is "term frequency of *canon* in title". Thus $\phi(q)$ becomes a query independent feature and $\Phi(q)$ becomes a feature query that can be executed in our inverted index by the Query Processor.

4 Learning for Structured Ranking

We now describe how we learn the domain dependent ranking function ρ, which is the core learning aspect of Object Search. As mentioned in the previous section, ρ differs from existing learning to rank work due to the structure in object queries. We exploit this structure to decompose the ranking function into several components (Section 4.1) and combine them using a probabilistic model. Existing learning to rank methods can then be leveraged to rank the individual components. Section 4.2 describes how we fit individual ranking scores into our probabilistic model by calibrating their probability.

4.1 Ranking model

As stated, ρ models the joint probability distribution over the space of documents and queries $\rho = P(d, q)$. Once estimated, this distribution can rank documents in $\mathcal{D}$ according to their probability of satisfying q. Since we are only interested in finding satisfying object pages, we introduce a variable ω which indicates if the document d is an object page. Furthermore, we introduce n variables ζ_i which indicate whether constraint c_i in the query q is satisfied. The probability computed by ρ is then:

$$\begin{aligned} P(d,q) &= P(\zeta_1,\ldots,\zeta_n,d) \\ &= P(\zeta_1,\ldots,\zeta_n,d,\omega) \\ &\quad +P(\zeta_1,\ldots,\zeta_n,d,\overline{\omega}) \\ &= P(d)P(\omega|d)P(\zeta_1,\ldots,\zeta_n|d,\omega) \\ &\quad +P(d)P(\overline{\omega}|d)P(\zeta_1,\ldots,\zeta_n|d,\overline{\omega}) \\ &= P(d)P(\omega|d)P(\zeta_1,\ldots,\zeta_n|d,\omega) \quad (2) \end{aligned}$$

$$\simeq P(\omega|d)\prod_{i=1}^{n} P(\zeta_i|d,\omega) \quad (3)$$

Equation 2 holds because non-object pages do not satisfy the query, thus, $P(\zeta_1,\ldots,\zeta_n|d,\overline{\omega}) = 0$. Equation 3 holds because we assume a uniform distribution over d and conditional independence over ζ_i given d and ω.

Thus, the rest of the problem is estimating $P(\omega|d)$ and $P(\zeta_i|d,\omega)$. The difference between these probability estimates lies in the features we use. Since ω depends only in d but not q, we use query independent features. Similarly, ζ_i only depends on d and c_i, thus we use features depending on c_i and d.

4.2 Calibrating ranking probability

In theory, we can use any learning algorithm mentioned in (Liu, 2009)'s survey to obtain the terms in Equation 3. In practice, however, such learning algorithms often output a ranking score that does not estimate the probability. Thus, in order to use them in our ranking model, we must transform that ranking score into a probability.

For empirical purposes, we use the *averaged* Perceptron (Freund and Schapire, 1999) to discriminatively train each component of the factored distribution independently. This algorithm requires a set of input vectors, which we obtain by applying the relational feature functions to the paired documents and queries. For each constraint c_i, we have a feature vector $\mathbf{x}_i = \Phi_i(d,q)$. The algorithm produces a weight vector of parameters $\mathbf{w}_i$ as output. The probability of c_i being satisfied by d given that d contains an object can then be estimated with a sigmoid function as:

$$P(c_i|d,\omega) \equiv P(true|\Phi_i(d,q)) \equiv \frac{1}{1+exp(-\mathbf{w}_i^{\mathsf{T}}\mathbf{x}_i)} \quad (4)$$

Similarly, to estimate $P(\omega|d)$, we use a feature vector that is dependent only on d. Denoting the function as Φ_0, we have $P(\omega|d) = P(true|\Phi_0(d,q))$, which can be obtained from (4).

While the sigmoid function has performed well empirically, probabilities it produces are not calibrated. For better calibrated probabilities, one can apply Platt scaling (Platt, 1999). This method introduces two parameters A and B, which can be computed using maximum likelihood estimation:

$$P(true|\Phi_i(d,q)) \equiv \frac{1}{1+exp(A\mathbf{w}_i^{\mathsf{T}}\Phi_i(d,q)+B)} \quad (5)$$

In contrast to the sigmoid function, Platt scaling can also be applied to methods that give un-normalized scores such as RankSVM (Cao et al., 2006).

Substituting (4) and (5) into (3), we see that our final learned ranking function has the form

$$\rho(d,q) = \prod_{i=0}^{n} \frac{1}{(1+exp(A_i\mathbf{w}_i^{\mathsf{T}}\Phi_i(d,q)+B_i))} \quad (6)$$

5 Learning Based Programming

Learning plays a crucial role in developing a new object domain. In addition to using supervised methods to learn ρ, we also exploit active learning to acquire training data from unlabeled web pages. The combination of these efforts would benefit from a unified framework and interface to machine learning. Learning Based Programming (LBP) (Roth, 2005) is such a principled framework. In this section, we describe how we applied and extended LBP to provide a user friendly interface for the developer to specify features and guide the learning process. Section 5.1 describes how we structured our framework around Learning Based Java (LBJ), an instance of LBP. Section 5.2 extends the framework to support interactive learning.

5.1 Learning Based Java

LBP is a programming paradigm for systems whose behaviors depend on naturally occurring data and that require reasoning about data and concepts in ways that are hard, if not impossible, to write explicitly. This is exactly our situation. Not only do we not know how to specify a ranking function for an object query, we might not even know exactly what features to use. Using LBP, we can specify abstract information sources that might contribute to decisions and apply a learning operator to them, thereby letting a learning algorithm figure out their importances in a data-driven way.

Learning Based Java (LBJ) (Rizzolo and Roth, 2007) is an implementation of LBP which we used and extended for our purposes. The most useful abstraction in LBJ is that of the *feature generation function* (FGF). This allows the programmer to reason in terms of feature *types*, rather than specifying individual features separately, and to treat them as native building blocks in a language for constructing learned functions. For example, instead of specifying individual features such as the phrases "professor of","product description", etc., we can specify a higher level feature type called "bigram", and let an algorithm select individual features for ranking purposes.

From the programming point of view, LBJ provides a clean interface and abstracts away the tedium of feature extraction and learning implementations. This enabled us to build our system quickly and shorten our development cycle.

5.2 Interactive Machine Learning

We advocate an interactive training process (Fails and Olsen, 2003), in which the developer iteratively improves the learner via two types of interaction (Algorithm 1).

The first type of interaction is similar to active learning where the learner presents unlabeled instances to the developer for annotation which it believes will most positively impact learning. In ranking problems, top ranked documents are presented as they strongly influence the loss function. The small difference from traditional active learning in our setting is that the developer assists this process by also providing more queries other than those encountered in the current training set.

The second type of interaction is feature selection. We observed that feature selection contributed significantly in the performance of the learner especially when training data is scarce. This is because with little training data and a huge feature space, the learner tends to over-fit. Fortunately in web search, the features used in ranking are in natural language and thereby intuitive to the developer. For example, one type of feature used in ranking the *university* constraint of a professor object query is the words surrounding the query field as in "university of ..." or "... university". If the learner only sees examples from the University of Anystate at Anytown, then it's likely that *Anytown* will have a high weight in addition to *University* and *of*. However, the *Anytown* feature will not generalize for documents from other universities. Having background knowledge like this, the developer can unselect such features. Furthermore, the fact that *Anytown* has a high weight is also an indication that the developer needs to provide more examples of other universities so that the learner can generalize (the first type of interaction).

Algorithm 1 Interactive Learning Algorithm

1: The developer uses keyword search to find and annotate an initial training set.
2: The system presents a ranked list of features computed from labeled data.
3: The developer adds/removes features.
4: The system learns the ranking function using selected features.
5: The developer issues queries and annotates top ranked unlabeled documents returned by the system.
6: If performance is not satisfactory, go to step 2.

The iterative algorithm starts with zero training data and continues until the learner's performance reaches a satisfactory point. At step 2, the developer is presented with a ranked list of features. To determine which features played the biggest role in the classifier's decision making, we use a simple ranking metric called *expected entropy loss* (Glover et al., 2001). Let f represent the event that a given feature is active. Let C be the event that the given example is classified as $true$. The conditional entropy of the classification distribution given that f occurs is $H(C|f) \equiv -P(C|f)\log(P(C|f)) - P(\overline{C}|f)\log(P(\overline{C}|f)$ and similarly, when f does not occur, we replace f by $\overline{f}$. The expected entropy loss is

$$\begin{aligned} L(C|f) &\equiv H(C) - \mathrm{E}[H(C|f)] \\ &= H(C) - (P(f)H(C|f) + \\ &\quad P(\overline{f})H(C|\overline{f}) \end{aligned} \tag{7}$$

The intuition here is that if the classification loses a lot of entropy when conditioned on a particular feature, that feature must be very discriminative and correlated with the classification itself.

It is noted that feature selection plays two important roles in our framework. First, it avoids overfitting when training data is scarce, thus increasing the effectiveness of our active learning protocol. Second, since search time depends on how many

domain	# pages	train	test
homepage	22.1	11.1	11
laptop	21	10.6	10.4
camera	18	9	9
random	97.8	48.9	48.8
total	158.9	79.6	79.2

Table 1: Number of web pages (in thousands) collected for experiment

features we use to query the web pages, keeping the number of features small will ensure that searching is fast enough to be useful.

Field	**Keywords**	**Example**
	Laptop domain	
brand	laptop,notebook	$lenovo$ laptop
processor	ghz, processor	2.2 ghz
price	$, price	$1000..1100
	Professor domain	
name	professor, research professor, faculty	research professor $scott$
university	university, university of	$stanford$ university

Table 2: Sample keyword reformulation for Google

6 Experimental Results

In this section we present an experiment that compares Object Search with keyword search engines.

6.1 Experimental Setting

Since we are the first to tackle this problem of answering structured query on the web, there is no known dataset available for our experiment. We collected the data ourselves using various sources from the web. Then we labeled search results from different object queries using the same annotation procedure described in Section 5.

We collected URLs from two main sources: the open directory (DMOZ) and existing search engines (SE). For DMOZ, we included URLs from relevant categories. For SE, we manually entered queries with keywords related to professors' homepages, laptops, and digital cameras, and included all returned URLs. Having collected the URLs, we crawled their content and indexed them. Table 1 summarizes web page data we have collected.

We split the data randomly into two parts, one for training and one for testing, and created a single inverted index for both of them. The developer can only see the training documents to select features and train ranking functions. At testing time, we randomly generate object queries, and evaluate on the testing set. Since Google's results come not from our corpus but the whole web, it might not be fair to compare against our small corpus. To accommodate this, we also added Google's results into our testing corpus. We believe that most 'difficult' web pages that hurt Google's performance would have been included in the top Google result. Thus, they are also available to test ours. In the future, we plan to implement a local IR engine to compare against ours and conduct a larger scale experiment to compare to Google.

We evaluated the experiment with two different domains: professor and laptop. We consider homepages and online shopping pages as object pages for the professor and laptop domains respectively.

For each domain, we generated 5 random object queries with different field configurations. Since Google does not understand structured queries, we reformulated each structured query into a simple keyword query. We do so by pairing the query field with several keywords. For example, a query field $a_{brand} \in \{lenovo\}$ can be reformulated as "lenovo laptop". We tried different combinations of keywords as shown in table 2. To deal with numbers, we use Google's advanced search feature that supports numeric range queries[1]. For example, a $price$ constraint $a_{price} \in [100, 200]$ might be reformulated as "price $100..200". Since it is too expensive to find the best keyword formulations for every query, we picked the combination that gives the best result for the first Google result page (Top 10 URLs).

6.2 Result

We measure the ranking performance with average precision. Table 3 shows the results for our search engine (OSE) and Google. Our ranking function outperforms Google for most queries, especially in

[1] A numeric range written as "100..200" is treated as a keyword that appears everywhere a number in the range appears

Qry	Professor		Laptop	
	OSE	Google	OSE	Google
1	**0.92** (71)	0.90(65)	**0.7** (15)	0.44 (12)
2	0.83(88)	**0.91**(73)	**0.62** (12)	0.26 (11)
3	0.51(73)	**0.66**(48)	**0.44** (40)	0.31 (24)
4	**0.42**(49)	0.3(30)	**0.36** (3)	0.09 (1)
5	**0.91**(18)	0.2(16)	**0.77** (17)	0.42 (3)

Table 3: Average precision for 5 random queries. The number of positive documents are in brackets

the laptop domain. In the professor domain, Google wins in two queries ("UC Berkeley professor" and "economics professors"). This suggests that in certain cases, reformulating to keyword query is a sensible approach, especially if all the fields in the object query are keywords. Even though Google can be used to reformulate some queries, it is not clear how and when this will succeed. Therefore, we need a principled solution as proposed in this paper.

7 Related Work

Many recent works propose methods for supporting structured queries on unstructured text (Jain et al., 2007), (Cafarella et al., 2007), (Gruhl et al., 2004). These works follow a typical extract-then-query approach, which has several problems as we discussed in section 1. (Agichtein, 2005) proposed using several large scale techniques. Their idea of using specialized index and search engine is similar to our work. However those methods assumes that structured data follows some textual patterns whereas our system can flexibly handle structured object using textual patterns as well as web page features.

Interestingly, the approach of translating structured queries to unstructured queries has been studied in (Liu et al., 2006). The main difference is that SEMEX relies on carefully hand-tuned heuristics on open-domain SQL queries while we use machine learning to do the translation on domain specific queries.

Machine Learning approaches to rank documents have been studied extensively in IR (Liu, 2009). Even though much of existing works can be used to rank individual constraints in the structured query. We proposed an effective way to aggregate these ranking scores. Further more, existing learning to rank works assumed a fixed set of features, whereas, the feature set in object search depends on object domain. As we have shown, the effectiveness of the ranking function depends much on the set of features. Thus, an semi-automatic method to learn these was proposed in section 5.

Our interactive learning protocol inherits features from existing works in Active Learning (see (Settles, 2009) for a survey). (Fails and Olsen, 2003) coined the term "interactive machine learning" and showed that a learner can take advantage of user interaction to quickly acquire necessary training data. (Roth and Small, 2009) proposed another interactive learning protocol that improves upon a relation extraction task by incremetally modifying the feature representation.

Finally, this work is related to document retrieval mechanisms used for question answering tasks (Voorhees, 2001) where precise retrieval methods are necessary to find documents which contain specific information for answering factoids (Agichtein et al., 2001).

8 Conclusion

We introduces the *Object Search* framework that searches the web for documents containing real-world objects. We formalized the problem as a learning to rank for IR problem and showed an effective method to solve it. Our approach goes beyond the traditional bag-of-words representation and views each web page as a set of domain independent features. This representation enabled us to rank web pages with respect to *object query*. Our experiments showed that, with small human effort, it is possible to create specialized search engines that outperforms GSEs on domain specific queries. Moreover, it is possible to search the web for documents with deeper meaning, such as those found in *object pages*. Our work is a small step toward semantic search engines by handling deeper semantic queries.

Acknowledgement

This work is supported by DARPA funding under the Bootstrap Learning Program, MIAS, a DHS-IDS Center for Multimodal Information Access and Synthesis at UIUC, NSF grant NSF SoD-HCER-0613885 and a grant from Yahoo! Inc.

References

Eugene Agichtein, Steve Lawrence, and Luis Gravano. 2001. Learning search engine specific query transformations for question answering. In *WWW '01: Proceedings of the 10th international conference on World Wide Web*, pages 169–178, New York, NY, USA. ACM.

Eugene Agichtein. 2005. Scaling Information Extraction to Large Document Collections. *IEEE Data Eng. Bull*, 28:3.

Michael Cafarella, Christopher Re, Dan Suciu, and Oren Etzioni. 2007. Structured Querying of Web Text Data: A Technical Challenge. In *CIDR*.

Yunbo Cao, Jun Xu, Tie-Yan Liu, Hang Li, Yalou Huang, and Hsiao-Wuen Hon. 2006. Adapting Ranking SVM to Document Retrieval. In *SIGIR '06: Proceedings of the 29th annual international ACM SIGIR conference on Research and development in information retrieval*, pages 186–193, New York, NY, USA. ACM.

Jerry Alan Fails and Dan R. Olsen, Jr. 2003. Interactive machine learning. In *IUI '03: Proceedings of the 8th international conference on Intelligent user interfaces*, pages 39–45, New York, NY, USA. ACM.

Yoav Freund and Robert E. Schapire. 1999. Large Margin Classification Using the Perceptron Algorithm. *Machine Learning*, 37(3):277–296.

Eric J. Glover, Gary W. Flake, Steve Lawrence, Andries Kruger, David M. Pennock, William P. Birmingham, and C. Lee Giles. 2001. Improving Category Specific Web Search by Learning Query Modifications. *Applications and the Internet, IEEE/IPSJ International Symposium on*, 0:23.

D. Gruhl, L. Chavet, D. Gibson, J. Meyer, P. Pattanayak, A. Tomkins, and J. Zien. 2004. How to Build a WebFountain: An Architecture for Very Large Scale Text Analytics. *IBM Systems Journal*.

A. Jain, A. Doan, and L. Gravano. 2007. SQL Queries Over Unstructured Text Databases. In *Data Engineering, 2007. ICDE 2007. IEEE 23rd International Conference on*, pages 1255–1257.

N. Kushmerick, D. Weld, and R. Doorenbos. 1997. Wrapper Induction for Information Extraction. In *IJCAI*, pages 729–737.

Jing Liu, Xin Dong, and Alon Halevy. 2006. Answering Structured Queries on Unstructured Data. In *WebDB*.

Tie-Yan Liu. 2009. Learning to Rank for Information Retrieval. *Found. Trends Inf. Retr.*, 3(3):225–331.

Andrew Kachites McCallum, Kamal Nigam, Jason Rennie, and Kristie Seymore. 2000. Automating the Construction of Internet Portals with Machine Learning. *Information Retrieval*, 3(2):127–163.

J. Platt. 1999. Probabilistic outputs for support vector machines and comparison to regularized likelihood methods. In *In Advances in Large Margin Classifiers*. MIT Press.

N. Rizzolo and D. Roth. 2007. Modeling Discriminative Global Inference. In *Proceedings of the First International Conference on Semantic Computing (ICSC)*, pages 597–604, Irvine, California, September. IEEE.

Dan Roth and Kevin Small. 2009. Interactive feature space construction using semantic information. In *CoNLL '09: Proceedings of the Thirteenth Conference on Computational Natural Language Learning*, pages 66–74, Morristown, NJ, USA. Association for Computational Linguistics.

Dan Roth. 2005. Learning Based Programming. *Innovations in Machine Learning: Theory and Applications*.

Burr Settles. 2009. Active learning literature survey. Computer Sciences Technical Report 1648, University of Wisconsin-Madison.

Ellen M. Voorhees. 2001. The trec question answering track. *Nat. Lang. Eng.*, 7(4):361–378.

Author Index

Association for Computational Linguistics
209 N. Eighth Street
Stroudsburg, Pennsylvania 18360

CURRAN ASSOCIATES INC
proceedings.com